STEALTH AIRCRAFT
ORIGAMI

JAYSON MERRILL

DOVER PUBLICATIONS
Garden City, New York

INTRODUCTION

Real-world aircraft don't always translate well to paper airplanes. Since they have their own type of physics, translating them into paper was both challenging and rewarding. Designing them forced me to alter my style and add many new techniques. Stealth aircraft have unusual shapes and achieving these shapes pushed me to rethink their design. I focused on the shapes, which forced me to engineer new folding techniques. Keeping these planes geometrically accurate while enabling them to fly was a challenge. I continue to implement what I've learned in new designs.

The exception to this is the Black Knight. It was 100 percent made for performance. I have flown this aircraft 237 feet, which is 11 feet farther than the record recorded by Guinness World Records in 2012. I did not use tape; the Black Knight has a double locking mechanism that keeps it together better than tape ever could. I wanted to fold stealth aircraft due to the lack of them in the origami community. This book is in no way for the beginner and only experts should attempt it. I hope that the reader will learn these techniques and use them to develop their own aircraft.

—Jayson Merrill

Copyright

Copyright © 2020 by Jayson Merrill
All rights reserved.

Bibliographical Note

Stealth Aircraft Origami is a new work,
first published by Dover Publications in 2020.

International Standard Book Number

ISBN-13: 978-0-486-82424-6
ISBN-10: 0-486-82424-1

Library of Congress Control Number
2019957183

Manufactured in the United States of America
82424105
www.doverpublications.com

TABLE OF CONTENTS

SYMBOLS AND SIGNS

PROCEDURES

BLACK KNIGHT

B-2 SPIRIT

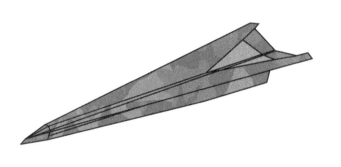

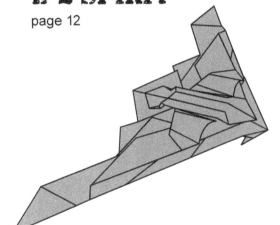

F-117 NIGHTHAWK

SR-71 BLACKBIRD

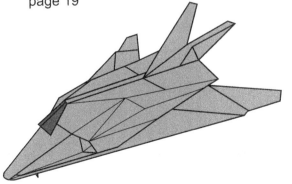

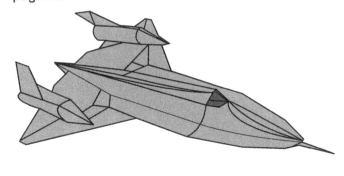

F-22 RAPTOR
page 37

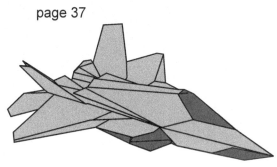

J-20 MIGHTY DRAGON
page 46

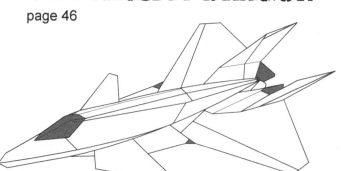

F-35 LIGHTNING
page 57

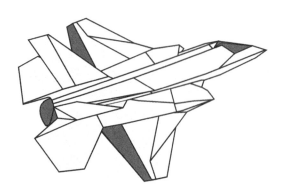

SUKHOI SU-57
page 69

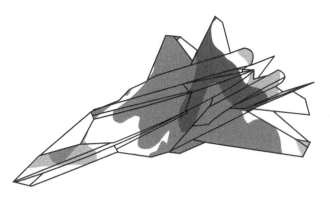

SYMBOLS AND SIGNS

Lines

——————————— This line indicates an edge.

·· This line indicates a hidden edge.

– – – – – – – – – – – This line indicates where to make a valley fold.

– · – · – · – · – · – This lines indicates where to make a mountain fold.

······································ This lines indicates a hidden fold.

Arrows

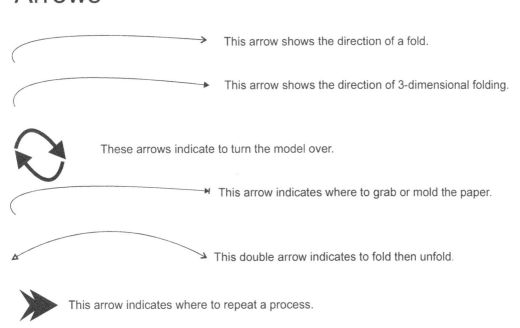

This arrow shows the direction of a fold.

This arrow shows the direction of 3-dimensional folding.

These arrows indicate to turn the model over.

This arrow indicates where to grab or mold the paper.

This double arrow indicates to fold then unfold.

This arrow indicates where to repeat a process.

PROCEDURES

Inside reverse fold

1.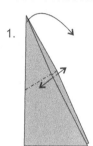

2.

Partially open the sides out and push the top in.

Outside reverse fold

1.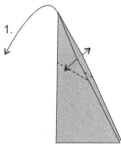

2.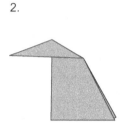

Partially open the sides out and push the top backward.

Squash fold

1.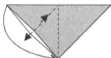

2.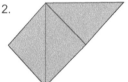

Pull the sides apart and push the corner down.

Rabbit ear fold

1.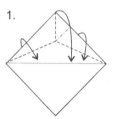

2.

3.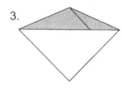

Push the two sides in and fold the corner over.

In progress.

Swivel fold

1.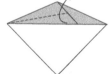

2.

3.

Pull the top layer up.

Continue to pull the layer until it lies flat. Push the area that stands up down.

Open sink

1.

2.

3.

Push the top in and partially open the paper.

Continue to push the top and push the sides in.

Preliminary fold

1.

2.

3.

Squash fold the flap down.

Closed sink

1.

2.

3.

Push the top in while keeping the paper together.

In progress.

4.

Turn the paper over.

5.

Squash fold the flap down.

6.

6

BLACK KNIGHT

The Black Knight is my interpretation of a mysterious object that some astronauts claim to have seen. It is most commonly reported as being triangular in shape and it's speculated that it is a U.F.O. or space debris. My plane doesn't resemble any aircraft. It is designed for performance only. I have thrown this plane 237 feet, which is 11 feet farther than the world record set in 2012.

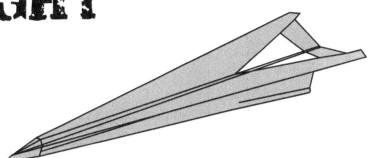

Use a sheet of 20–28 lb. A4 paper.

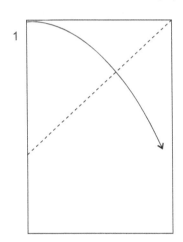

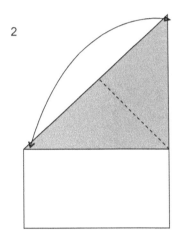

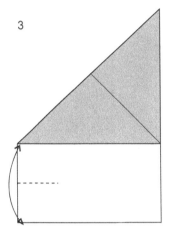

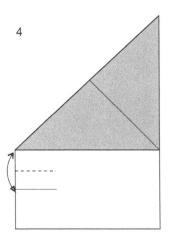

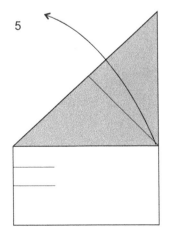

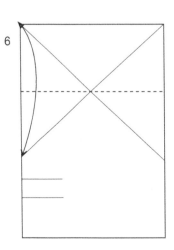

7

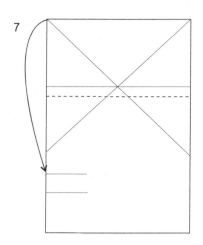

8

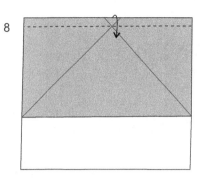

9

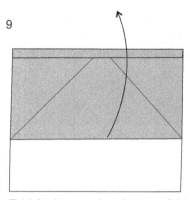

Fold the layer up but do not unfold the crease made in step 8.

10

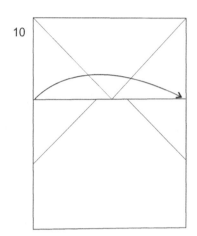

11

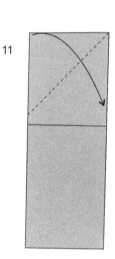

12

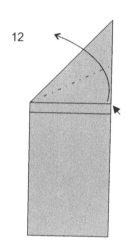

13

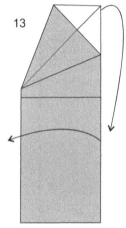

Fold the side edge out and fold the top edge in as shown.

14

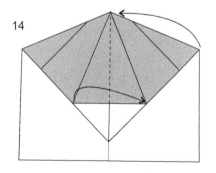

15

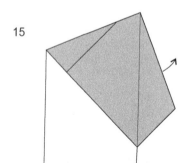

16

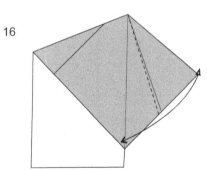

Fold then unfold the flap over slightly beyond the line shown. This will compensate for the thickness of the paper later.

17

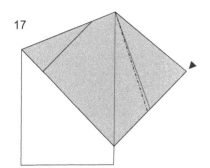

18

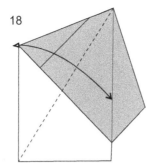

19

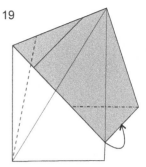

Mountain fold the flap in, divide the long edge in thirds and valley fold it over.

20

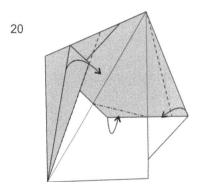

Fold the long edge over, mountain fold the small area under, and divide the right edge into thirds and valley fold it over. Leave a small space near the tip to compensate for the thickness of the paper.

21

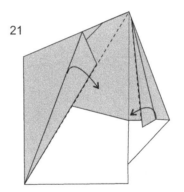

22

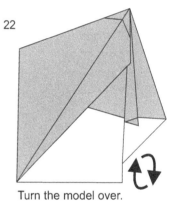

Turn the model over.

23

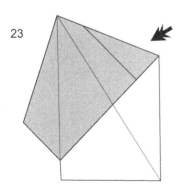

Repeat steps 18–23 to this side.

24

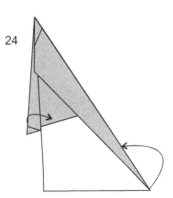

Fold one large layer forward and fold one small triangle backward.

25

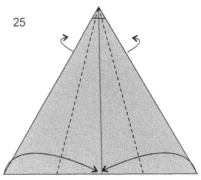

Fold the edges in and swing the rear edges out.

26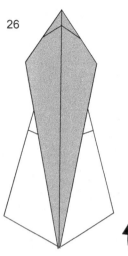

Turn the model over.

27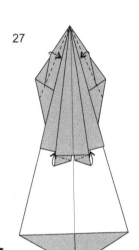

28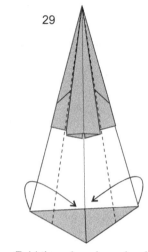

29

Fold the edges in and swing the rear edges out.

30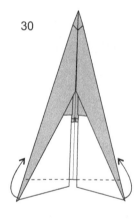

31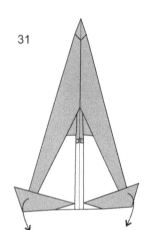

Unfold these folds, then inside reverse fold the edges underneath the layers behind so that the wings lock into themselves.

32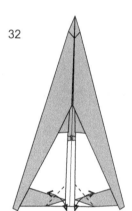

33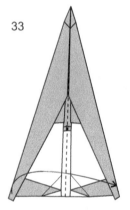

34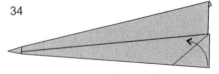

Using the small white triangular pockets formed in step 32 place one flap into the other, then fold the layers over together.

35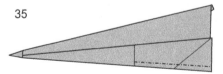

Round the area. This makes it easier to balance the plane.

36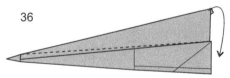

Fold the wings down as shown.

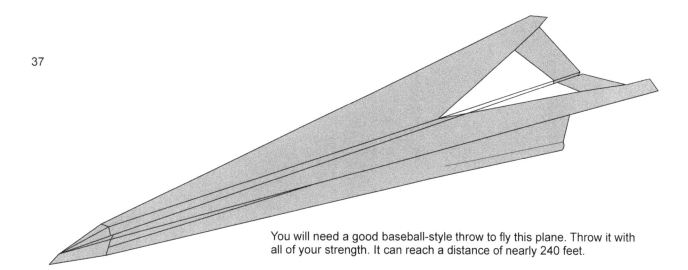

You will need a good baseball-style throw to fly this plane. Throw it with all of your strength. It can reach a distance of nearly 240 feet.

B-2 SPIRIT

The B-2 Spirit has its design roots in World War II with the Horten flying wing. Official development was started in 1979. The B-2 is a long range stealth bomber capable of flying great distances and delivering nuclear weapons. It has seen combat in Kosovo, Afghanistan, and Iraq. It remains in service to this day.

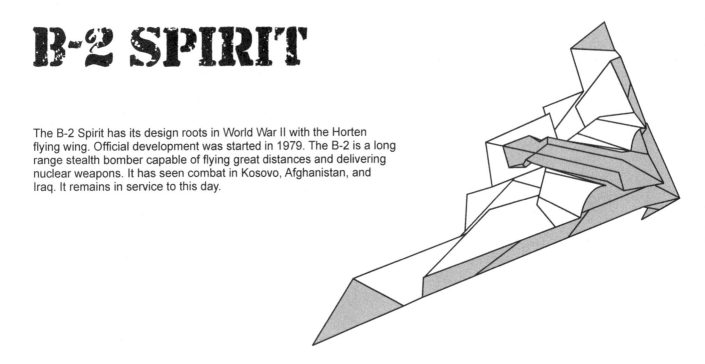

Use an 11-inch-square sheet of foil paper.

1

Make the creases as shown.

2

3

Turn the model over.

4

5

Unfold the model to step 1.

6

Fold then unfold.

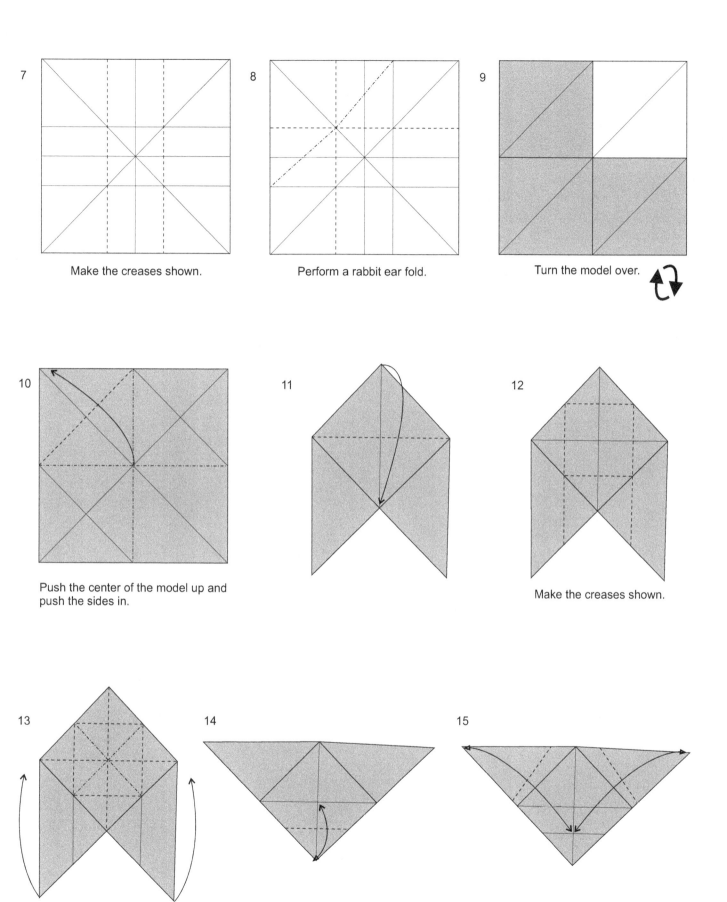

7

Make the creases shown.

8

Perform a rabbit ear fold.

9

Turn the model over.

10

Push the center of the model up and push the sides in.

11

12

Make the creases shown.

13

Push the center section in and swing the large flaps up.

14

15

13

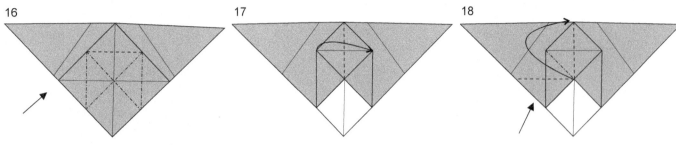

16 Squash the area in, forming a preliminary fold.

17

18 Push the center edge up and fold the side in.

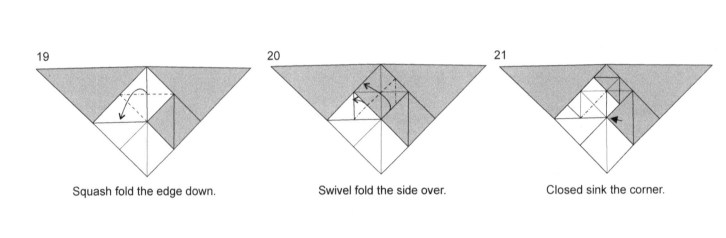

19 Squash fold the edge down.

20 Swivel fold the side over.

21 Closed sink the corner.

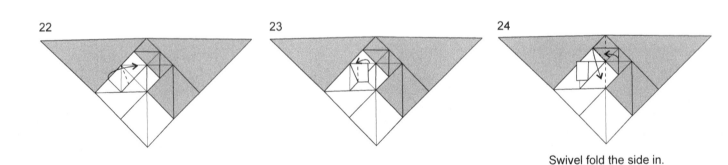

22

23

24 Swivel fold the side in.

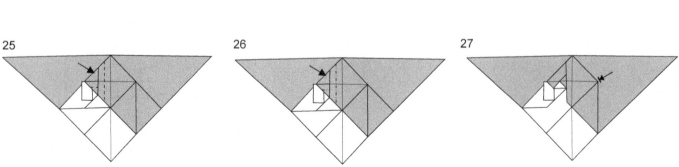

25 Swivel fold the side in, then back to form creases.

26 Open sink the side in using the creases.

27 Repeat steps 17–27 to this side.

28

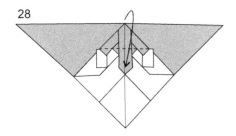

29

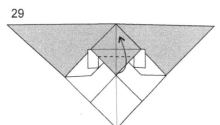

30

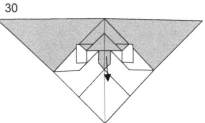

Pull the flap down. You will need to refold a few edges inside to flatten the layer.

31

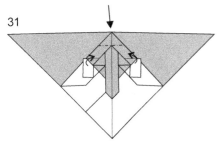

Open sink the corner. Bring the flaps from behind to the front.

32

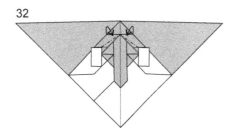

Mountain fold the edges in.

33

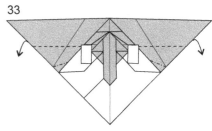

Using the creases made in step 15 as a guide, crimp the flaps down.

34

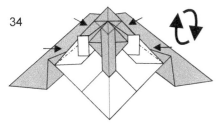

Fold the inner triangle made from the closed sink up, mountain fold the edges in, then turn the model over.

35

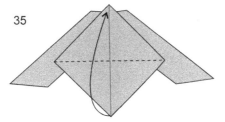

36

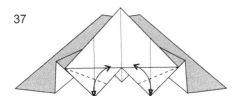

Fold then unfold the corners. Bring the layer from behind to the front.

37

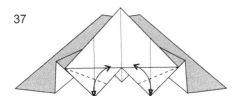

Fold then unfold the edges.

38

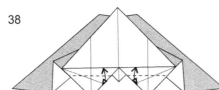

Using the creases just made, fold then unfold the flaps.

39

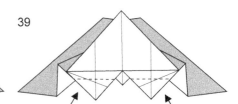

Using the creases just made, inside reverse fold the flaps in and out as shown.

40

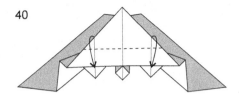

Using the creases as a guide, fold the flap down.

41

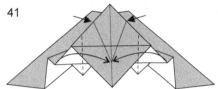

Fold the inside edges to the center, fold the flaps in.

42

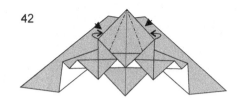

Mountain fold the edges in.

43

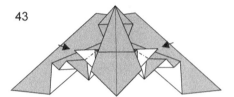

Squash fold the flaps in.

44

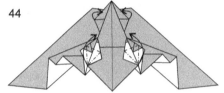

Petal fold the flaps, then mountain fold the top edges in.

45

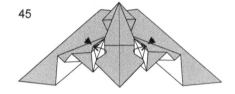

Fold the small edges in, then fold the flaps in half.

46

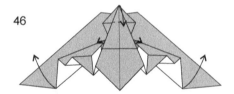

Inside reverse fold the flaps out, swivel fold the edges out as shown, and fold the point down.

47

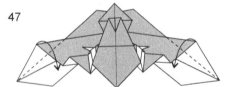

48

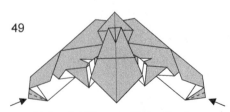

Inside reverse fold the wingtips in.

49

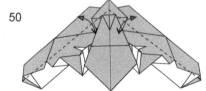

Valley fold the small wingtips in.

50

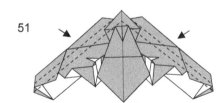

Fold then unfold the sides as shown.

51

Roll the edges in and perform a rabbit ear fold.

52

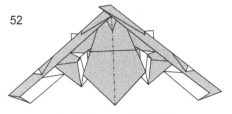

Fold the model in half.

53

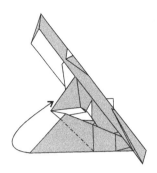

Inside reverse fold the flap in.

54

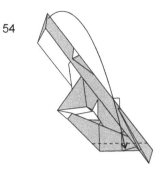

Fold the wings down as shown.

55

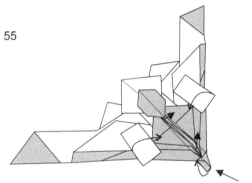

Fold the air intakes over, pop the
fuselage out, then inside reverse fold the
nose in to lock the model.

56

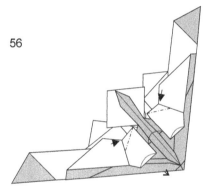

First fold the back edges of the
air intakes to lock them into place before
rounding them, round the fuselage, and
slide the front landing strut down.

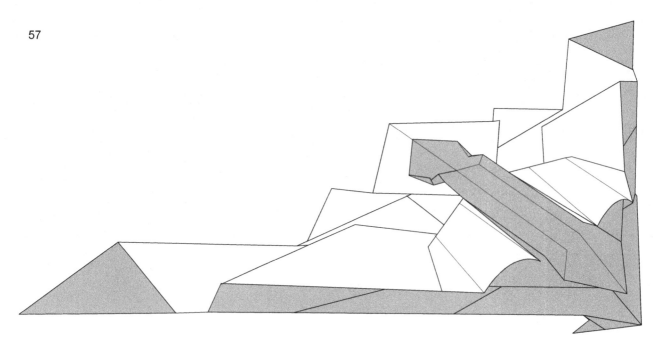

To fly this plane, slightly bend the wings up, inside reverse fold the rear landing gear, fold the forward landing strut forward. It is difficult to balance and you will need to bend the trailing edges up. Give it a gentle throw. It is designed to be a glider so it is slow and maneuverable.

F-117 NIGHTHAWK

The F-117 was developed by Lockheed Martin in the early 1980s. It was developed in Area 51 secretly and wasn't revealed to the public until 1988. It saw combat in the 1991 Gulf War and other conflicts. Although it is known as a stealth fighter, it is not a fighter. Its role is primarily as a precision bomber. It was retired in 2008 after the F-22 was fielded.

Use a 13- to 15-inch-square sheet of thin, strong paper.

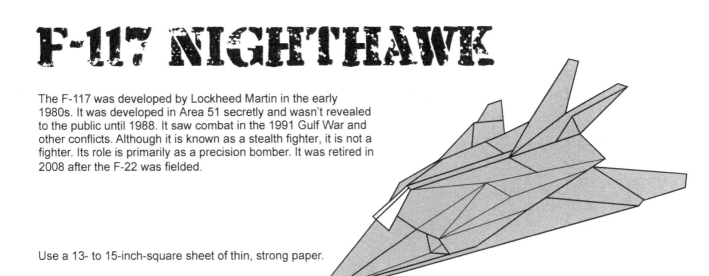

1

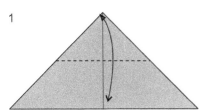

Begin with a waterbomb base. Fold then unfold the point down.

2

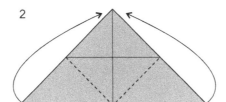

3

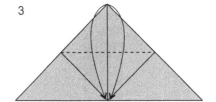

4

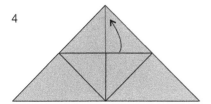

Pull the trapped paper from underneath out.

5

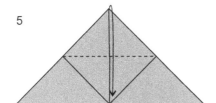

6

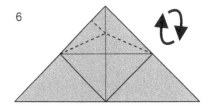

Rabbit ear fold the flap then turn the model over.

7

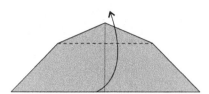

Fold the bottom of the triangle up.

8

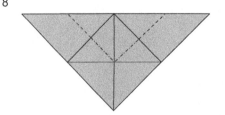

Squash fold the areas shown.

9

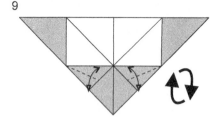

Fold then unfold the edges shown, then turn the model over.

10

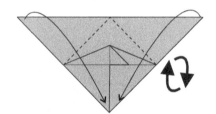

Fold the flaps down, then turn the model over.

11

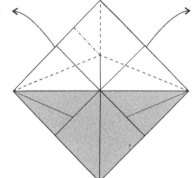

Rabbit ear fold the top triangle and swing the rear flaps out.

12

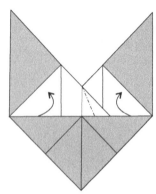

Squash fold the center triangle, then pull the trapped paper from underneath out.

13

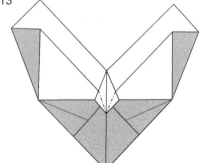

Petal fold the small flap.

14

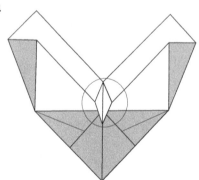

The next series of steps will focus on the center flap.

15

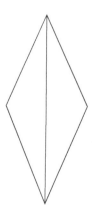

Fold then unfold as shown.

16
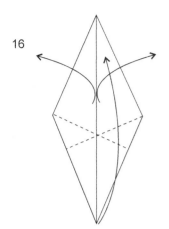

Rabbit ear fold the flap down and pull the top edges out.

17
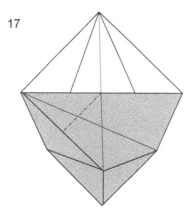

Inside reverse fold the flap in.

18
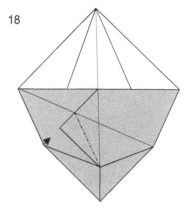

Squash fold the flap.

19
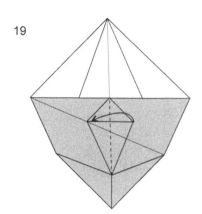

20
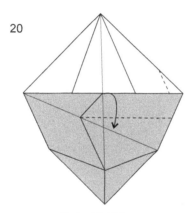

Swivel fold the area down.

21
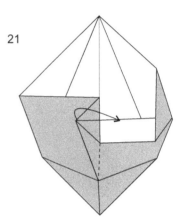

Fold two layers over.

22
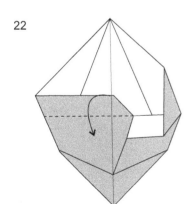

Swivel fold the area down.

23
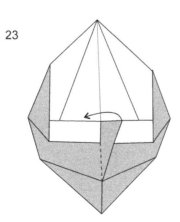

Fold one layer over. The next series of steps will focus on the rest of the model.

24
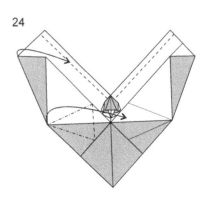

First fold then unfold 1/3 of the sides shown in, then petal fold the flap over and down.

25

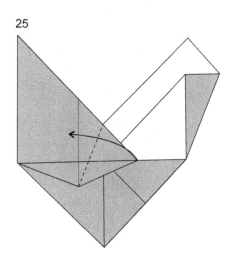

26

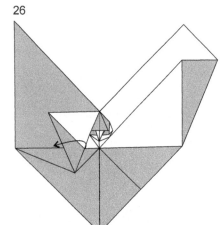

27

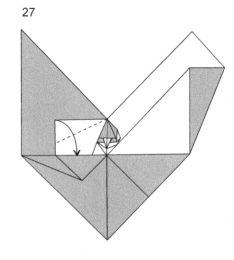

28

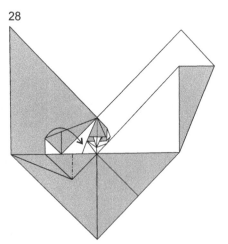

Swivel the edge in and swing
the bottom edge out.

29

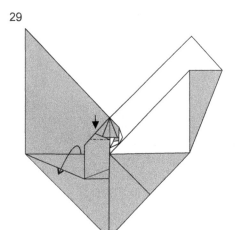

Inside reverse fold the small
area in. Pull the trapped
layers out.

30

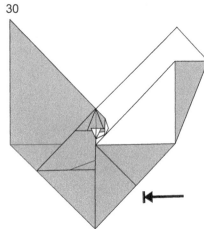

Repeat steps 24–30 to this
side.

31

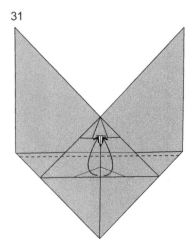

Fold the edges up using the
small lines as shown.

32

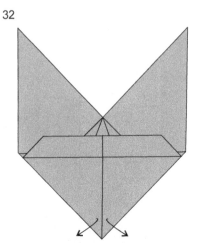

Shift the flaps down using
the folds just made.

33

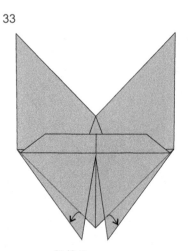

Shift the paper
underneath out.

34

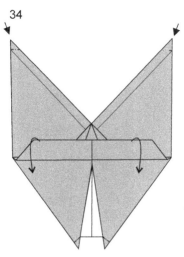

Fold the edges down.
Inside reverse fold the small
tips in on the four flaps.

35

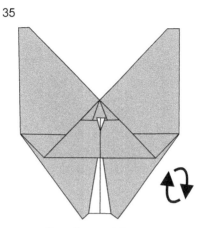

Turn the model over.

36

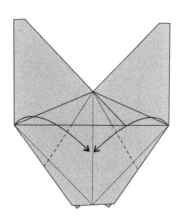

Using the inner edge
fold the sides in as
shown. Note this will
form a swivel fold.

37

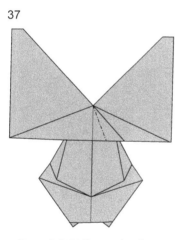

Squash fold the center flap.

38

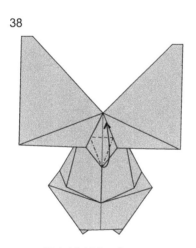

Petal fold the flap up.

39

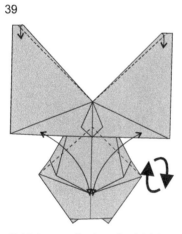

Fold the small edges in, fold then
unfold the flaps over, then turn
the model over.

40

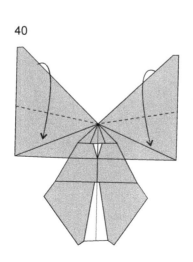

41

42

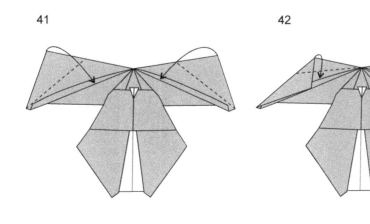

43

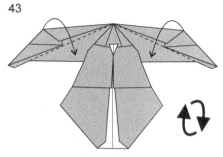

Fold the wings down, then turn the model over.

44

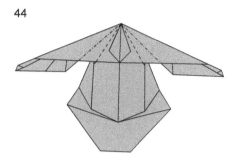

Crimp the wings as shown.

45

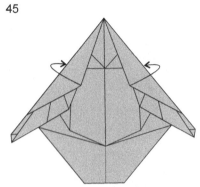

Pull the paper out and wrap it around the edge of the wing.

46

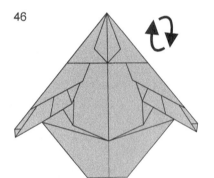

Turn the model over.

47

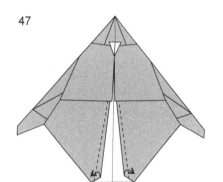

48

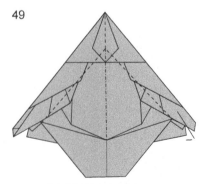

Fold the tailfins out, then turn the model over.

49

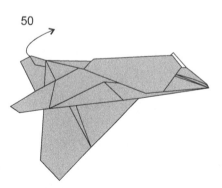

Jet fold the model.

50

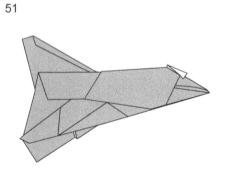

Shift the jet fold up using step 51 as a reference.

51

Unfold the model to step 49.

24

52

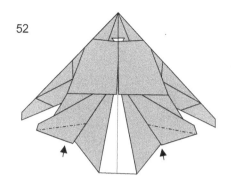

Inside reverse fold the edges in, but leave a small portion of the back edges on the other side of the crease made in step 51 so it doesn't overlap.

53

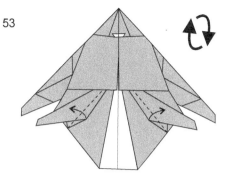

Fold the edges up, then turn the model over.

54

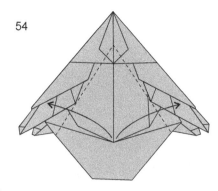

55

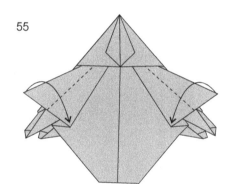

56

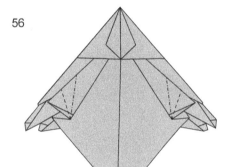

Inside reverse fold the flaps into thirds.

57

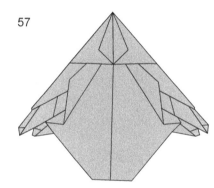

Return the model to step 51.

58

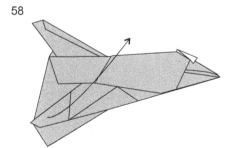

Open the model out.

59

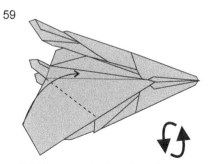

Fold the area in, then turn the model over.

60

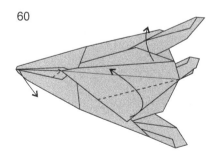

Fold the edge over, inside reverse fold the front flap in, fold the rear landing struts out, then reposition the model as shown in step 61.

61

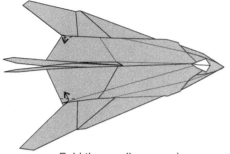

Fold the small corners in as shown.

62

Open up the edges.

63

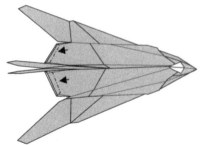

Push in the areas to form the engines as shown.

64

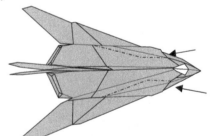

Open out the engines and shape the fuselage as shown.

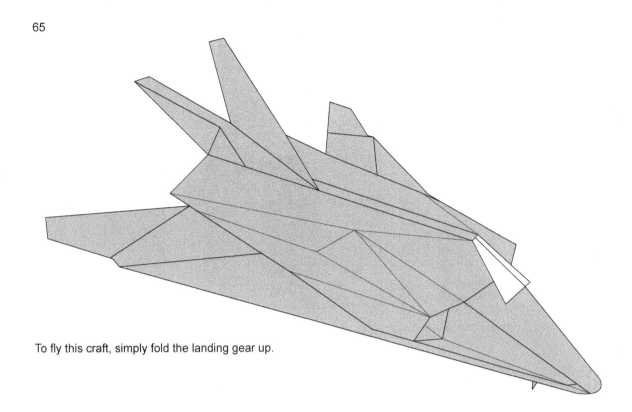

To fly this craft, simply fold the landing gear up.

SR-71 BLACKBIRD

The SR-71 Blackbird was developed in the 1960s as a reconnaissance aircraft. It flew over Soviet airspace and was never shot down. The jet could fly at speeds over Mach 3. It was one of the first aircraft to have a reduced radar cross section.

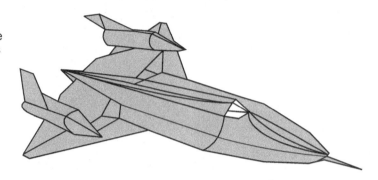

Use a 13-inch-square sheet of foil paper or thin paper.

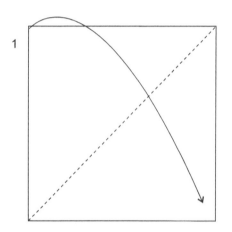

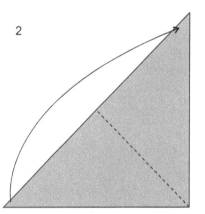

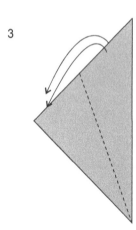

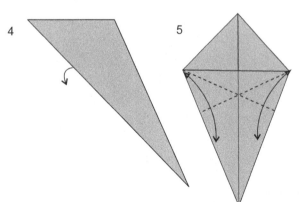

Unfold to step 2.

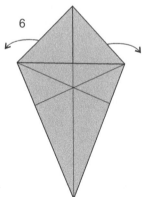

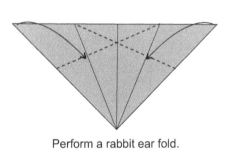

Perform a rabbit ear fold.

8

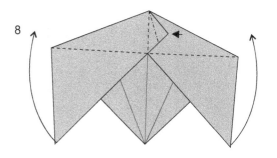

9

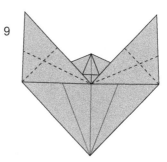

Make the creases shown.

10

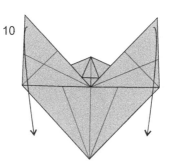

11

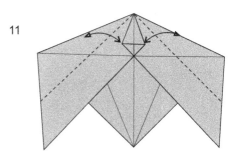

12

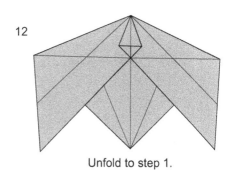

Unfold to step 1.

13

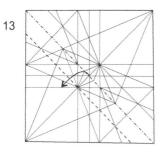

14

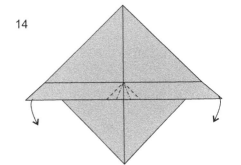

Using the creases crimp the center
area and bring the outer edges in.

15

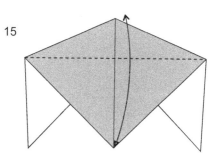

16

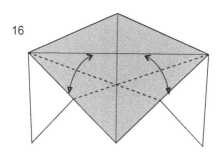

17

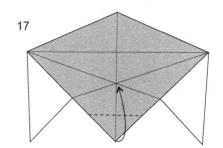

18

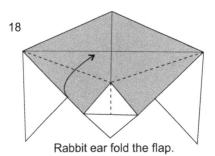

Rabbit ear fold the flap.

19

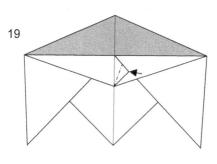

20

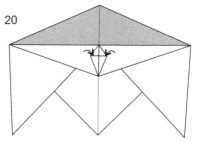

Wrap the paper from underneath around.

21

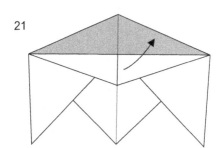

Pull the top layer up.

22

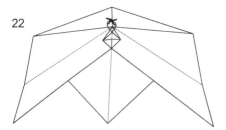

Insert the edges into the area shown then close the model.

23

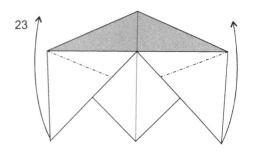

24

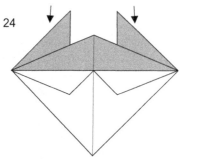

Inside reverse fold the flaps down.

25

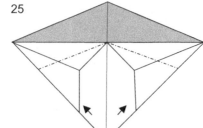

Squash fold the flaps in.

26

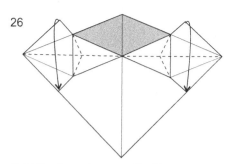

Fold the flaps down and inside reverse fold the small areas in as shown.

27

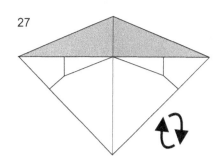

Turn the model over.

28

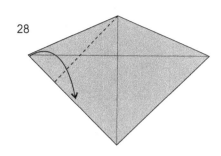

29

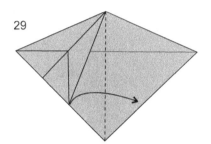

Pull the trapped paper over.

30

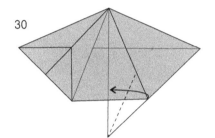

31

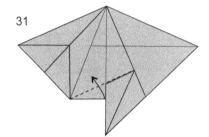

32

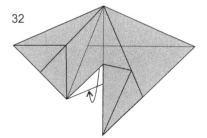

Wrap the paper underneath.

33

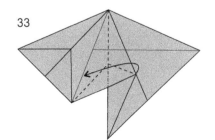

Fold the side over and in as shown.

34

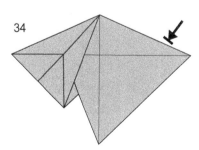

Repeat steps 28–34 to this side.

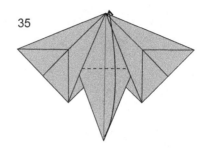

35

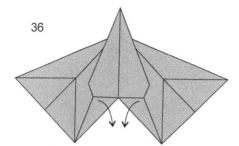

36

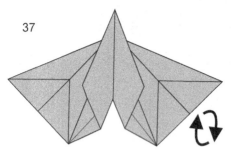

37

Turn the model over.

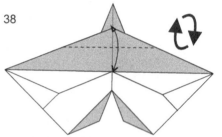

38

Fold then unfold the area shown,
then turn the model over.

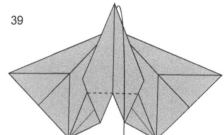

39

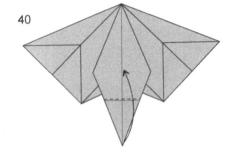

40

41

Turn the model over.

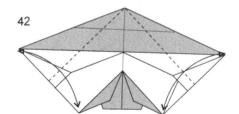

42

43

Using the small fold made in step 26
pull the flaps behind out and restructure
them as shown.

44

Note the top angle of the flaps that you just pulled out.

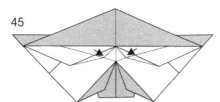

45

Shift the edge out using the lines as a guide.

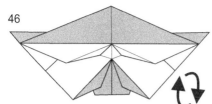

46

Turn the model over.

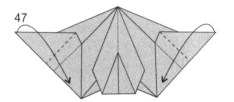

47

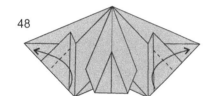

48

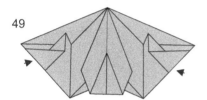

49

Inside reverse fold these flaps using the creases just made.

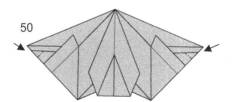

50

Inside reverse fold the tips in.

51

Inside reverse fold the tips in.

52

Closed sink these edges in.

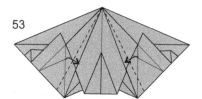

53 Crimp the intersection shown to the edge.

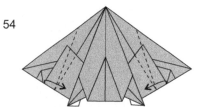

54 First fold the engines over then fold the wings in using the intersections shown in step 55.

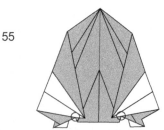

55 Note how the edges of the wings touch the intersection. Return the wings to step 54.

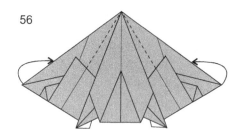

56

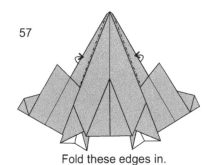

57 Fold these edges in.

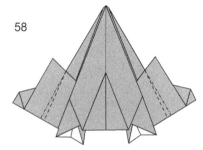

58 Crimp the engines in so that they lie perpendicular to the edge. This will allow the plane to fly straight.

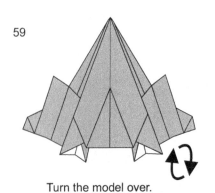

59 Turn the model over.

60 Fold the wings over using the folds made in step 54 as a guide and box pleat the paper that pops up.

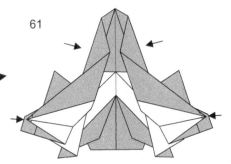

61 Inside reverse fold the edges in. You will have to unlock the paper underneath first. Then inside reverse fold the wing tips in.

62

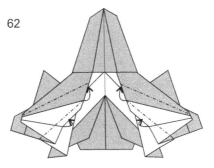

Fold the edges of the wings in, then lock the wings to the engines by folding the rear edges of the wings in.

63

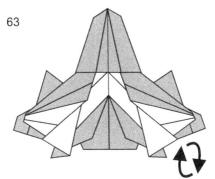

Turn the model over.

64

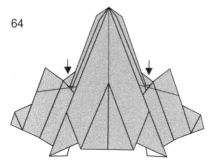

Fold the inner edges in as far as they will go.

65

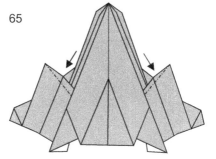

Fold both sets of edges in as far as they will go, you will have to unlock the edges first.

66

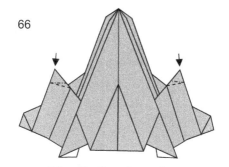

Crimp the flaps in as shown.

67

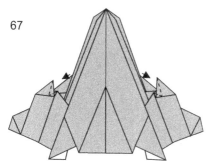

Crimp the edges in as shown.

68

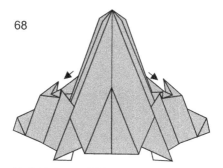

Unfold then refold the engines using the creases you just made.

69

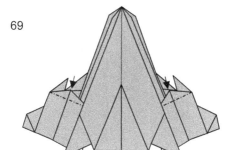

Fold the edges in front and back.

70

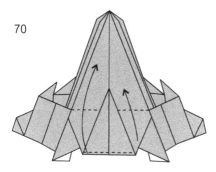

Using the crease fold the flap up and slide it up until the edges meet the edges underneath it.

71

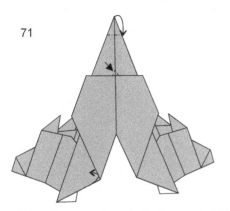

Wrap the paper from behind around, fold the tip behind, slightly fold the excess paper out at the pleat to form a cockpit.

72

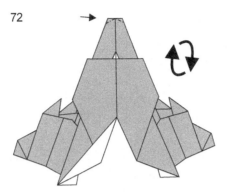

Mountain fold the edges behind, then turn the model over.

73

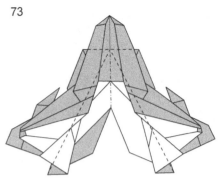

Jet fold the model.

74

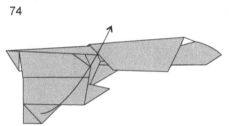

Open out the side of the model.

75

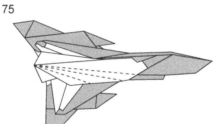

Divide the layer into 1/4th and roll it over. Close the model.

76

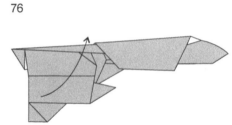

Fold the wings up and gently fold the forward area.

77

Fold the engines up and round them, thin the nose, give the fuselage a round slope and fold the edges into the fuselage to lock it into place. Finally, roll the rear edges to shape the tail boom.

78

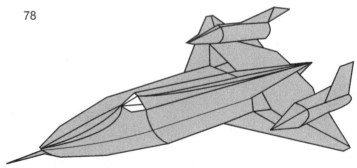

Throw this plane with some force. It can fly up to 100 feet.

F-22 RAPTOR

In 1981 the United States military began development of a fifth-generation fighter designed to replace the F-15. This program led to the F-22 Raptor as it is now known. This aircraft's primary mission is to engage air targets and achieve air dominance. Russia and China have started their own programs to counter the F-22. The F-22 has seen combat in Syria. The United States has forbidden sales of this aircraft to other countries including its allies due to the classified technology it incorporates.

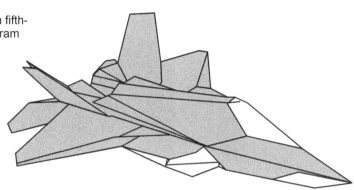

Use an 8½-inch square of any type paper.

1

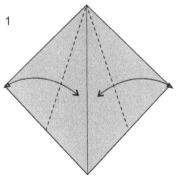

Begin with a preliminary fold.
Fold then unfold the sides in.

2

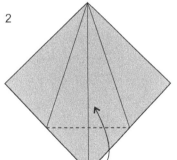

3

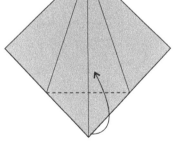

4

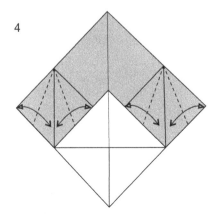

5

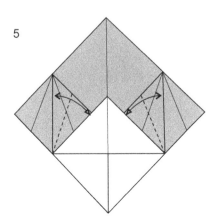

6

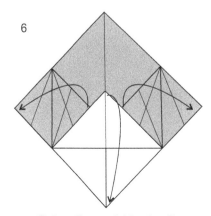

Return the model to step 2.

7

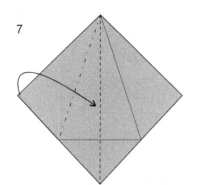

8

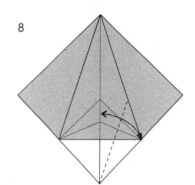

9

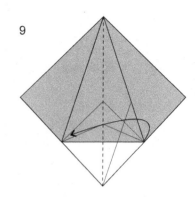

10

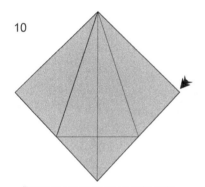

Repeat steps 7–9 on this side.

11

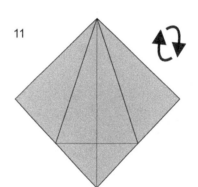

Turn the model over.

12

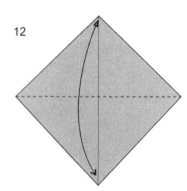

13

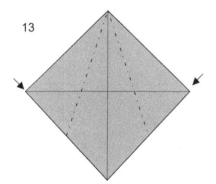

Squash fold the sides in.

14

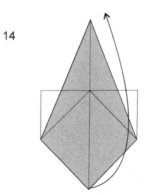

Using the pre-existing creases squash fold the flap up.

15

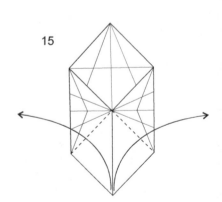

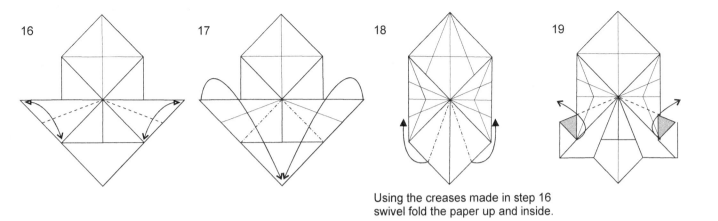

18 Using the creases made in step 16 swivel fold the paper up and inside.

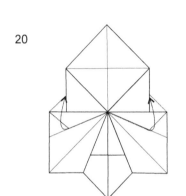

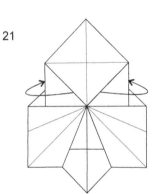

20 Mountain fold the flaps behind up as shown.

21 Perform a closed wrap with the paper shown.

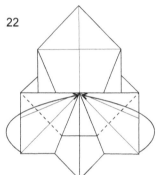

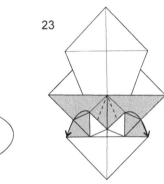

23 Squash fold the flaps down.

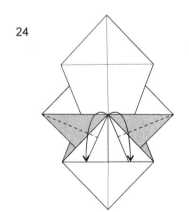

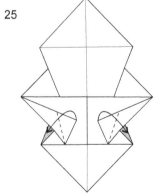

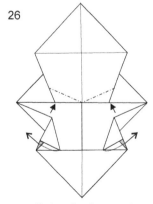

26 Swing the flaps out. Then sink the corners in.

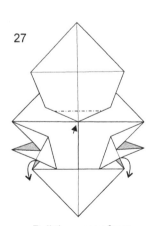

27 Pull the paper from underneath out as shown. Open sink the corner in.

28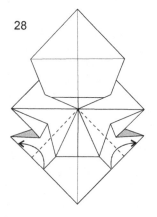

29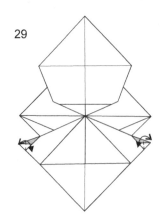

30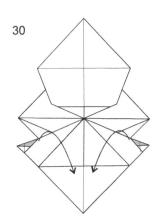

31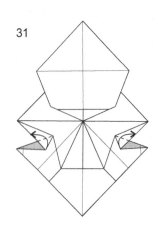

32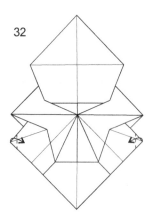

33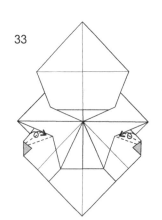

34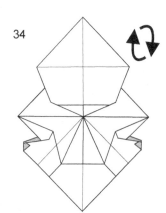

Turn the model over.

35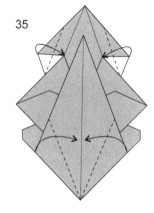

36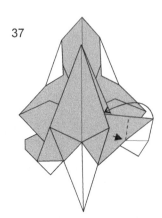

Swivel fold the flap up.
The model will not lie
flat.

37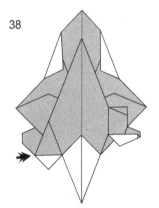

Push this area in, swing the
flap over, and flatten it out
as shown in step 38.

38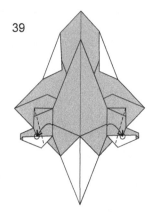

Repeat steps 36–38
to this flap.

39

Fold the edges of the flaps
to the intersections shown.

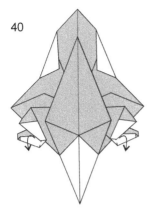

40

Swivel fold the flaps down as shown.

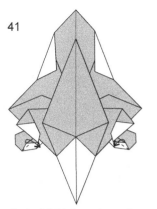

41

Swivel fold the edges down.

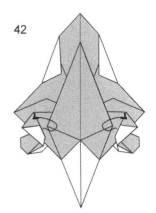

42

Move the layer of paper from underneath to the top.

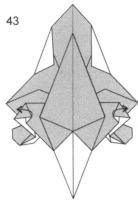

43

Swivel the small layers of paper over.

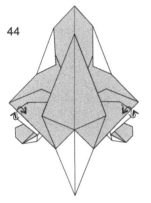

44

Fold the top layer down while simultaneously folding the back layer up.

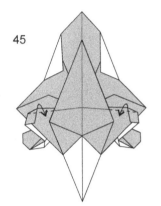

45

Fold the layer of paper down as shown.

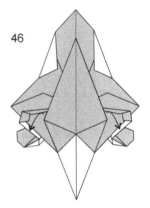

46

Using the crease you just made slide the paper down.

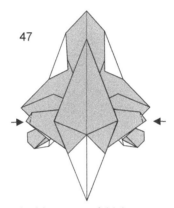

47

Inside reverse fold the tips in.

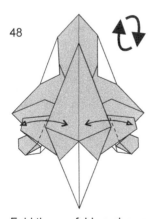

48

Fold then unfold as shown, then turn the model over.

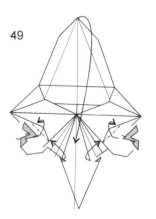

49

Petal fold the top flap down. Mountain fold the small triangles under. Swivel fold the bottom edges back along their original creases.

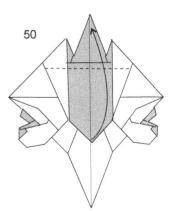

50

51

Reposition the top layer of paper into the pocket behind it.

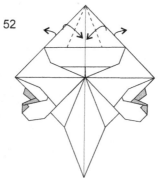

52

Swivel fold the side layers over then allow the layers behind to swing out as shown in step 53.

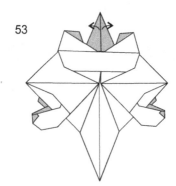

53

Slightly swivel the layers out. You will need this excess paper to lock the nose together.

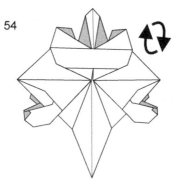

54

Turn the model over.

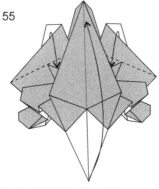

55

Swivel fold the two side edges in, then petal fold the bottom flap up. You will have to swivel fold the sides in at the bottom of the petal fold. Use the next step as a reference.

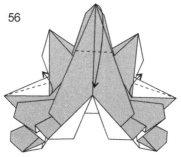

56

Fold the top flap down. Fold the edges ⅔ of the angle up to cover the leading edges of the wings.

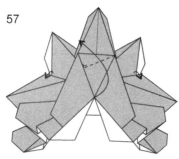

57

Fold the top flap up perpendicular to the side. Swivel fold some paper from the sides to the top as shown.

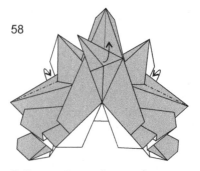

58

Pull some trapped paper from underneath out. Mountain fold the edges under.

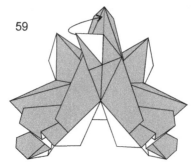

59

Unfold to step 57.

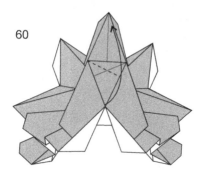

60

Repeat steps 57–59 to this side.

61

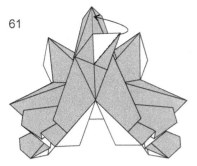

Swivel fold the flap over.

62

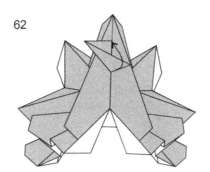

63

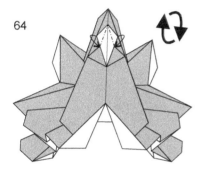

Squash fold the flap down.

64

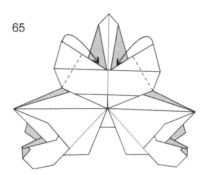

Mountain fold the sides in,
then turn the model over.

65

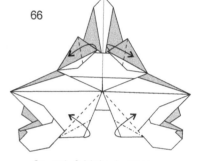

66

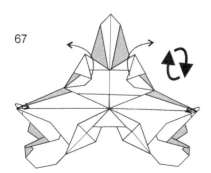

Squash fold the bottom
flaps. Fold the top flaps
over as shown.

67

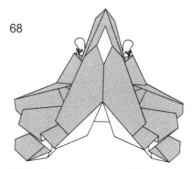

Unfold to step 65 then closed
sink the areas shown.
Inside reverse fold the tips in.
Turn the model over.

68

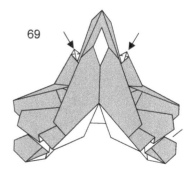

Using the creases made in
step 66, fold the flaps in.

69

Inside reverse fold the small
edges in.

70

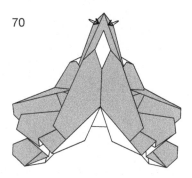

Valley fold the small excess edges in.

71

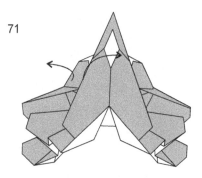

Open the side of the model.

72

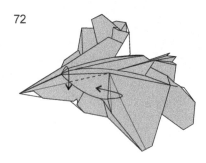

Carefully slide the excess paper on the wing forward then close the model as shown.

73

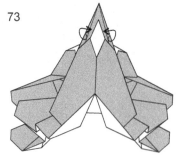

Roll the flap you just created in thirds over on the inside of the model.

74

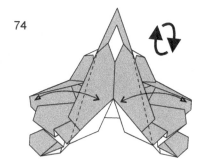

Fold then unfold the wings in, then turn the model over.

75

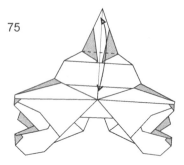

Fold then unfold the flap as shown.

76

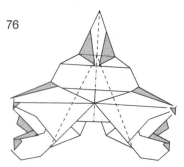

Jet fold the model as shown.

77

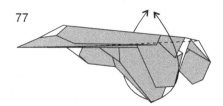

Fold the wings up.

78

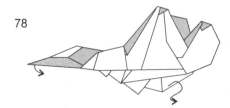

Pull the layers in the nose out. Place one of the rear edges into the pocket behind, then fold them together to lock the model.

79

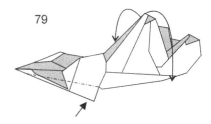

Inside reverse fold the
bottom area in as shown,
then fold the wings down.

80

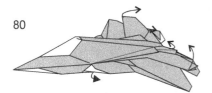

Fold the tailfins up. Open the
air intakes and shape the
engines.

81

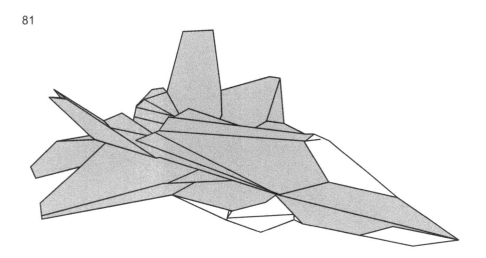

Give this plane a hard throw. It can fly up to 115 feet with good maneuverability.

J-20 MIGHTY DRAGON

The Chengdu J-20 Mighty Dragon was developed by China in the 1990s and was completed in 2011. It was developed as an air superiority fighter. It has not seen any combat and it remains in service.

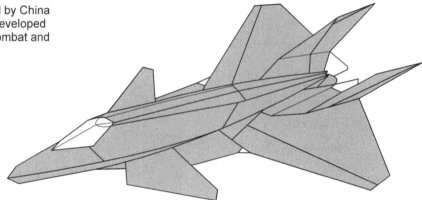

Use a 13-inch-square sheet of foil paper.

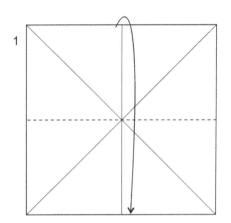

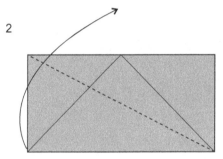

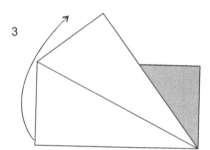

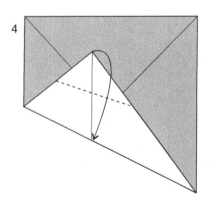

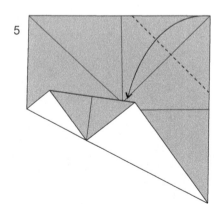

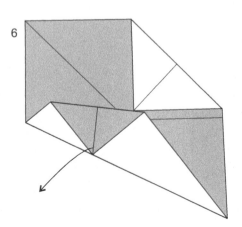

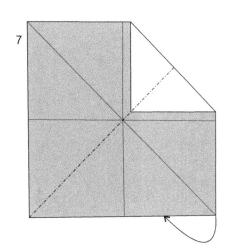

7

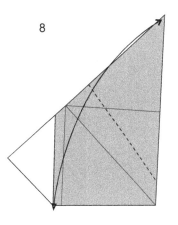

8

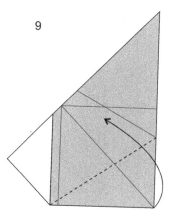

9

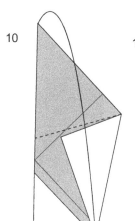

10

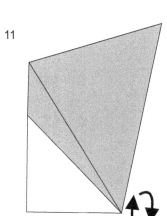

11

Turn the model over.

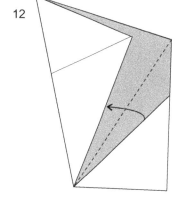

12

Fold the edge over to the line shown.

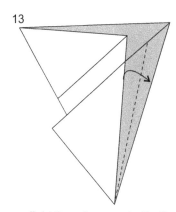

13

Fold the edge over to the line shown.

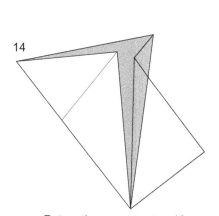

14

Return the paper to step 10.

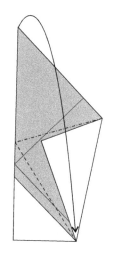

15

Open the paper along the creases shown.

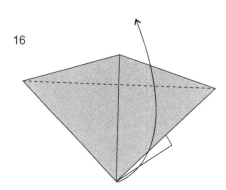

16

17

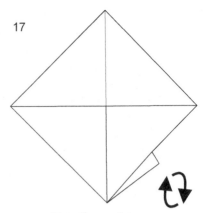

Turn the model over.

18

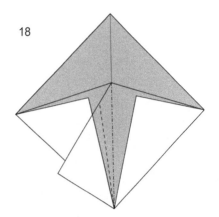

Inside reverse fold the edge along the creases shown.

19

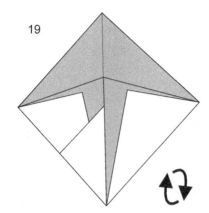

Turn the model over.

20

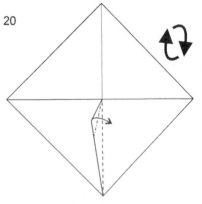

Squash fold the area over, then turn the model over.

21

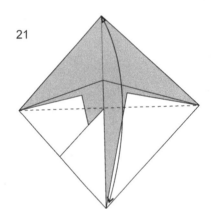

Fold then unfold the flap.

22

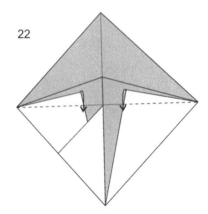

23

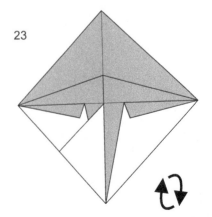

Turn the model over.

24

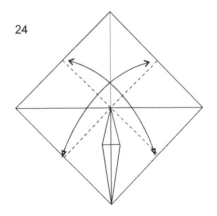

Fold then unfold the creases shown.

25

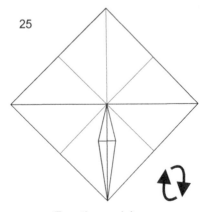

Turn the model over.

26

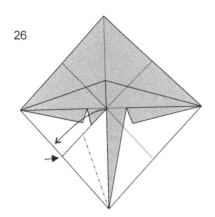

Inside reverse fold the edge and swing the layer of trapped paper out.

27

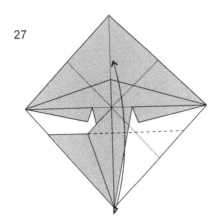

28

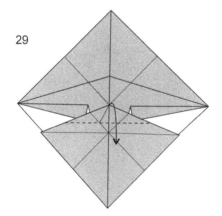

Fold the area on the small triangle out, then swing the layers up as shown in step 29.

29

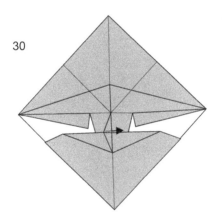

Perform a modified petal fold.

30

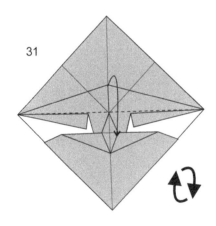

Pull the trapped paper out.

31

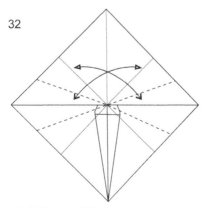

Fold the flap down, then turn the model over.

32

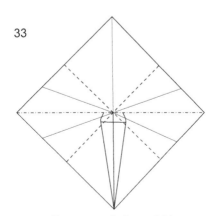

Fold then unfold the creases shown.

33

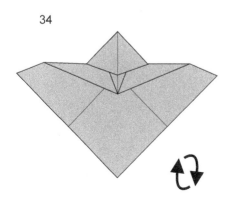

Form a preliminary fold.

34

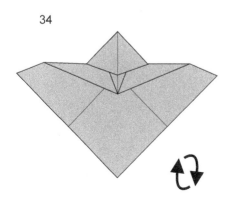

Turn the model over.

49

35
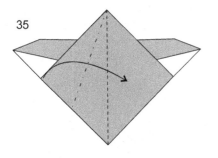

36
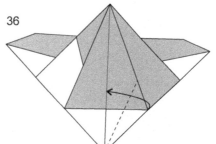

37
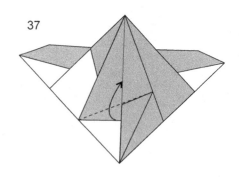

38
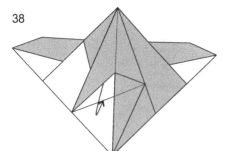

Fold the edge underneath.

39
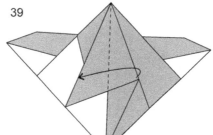

40
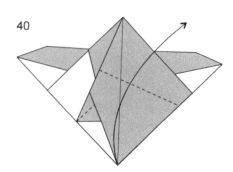

Fold the flap up and swivel the edge over.

41
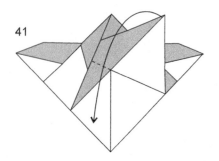

42

Repeat steps 35–42 to this side.

43
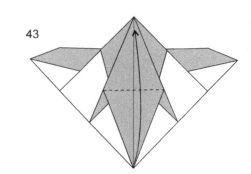

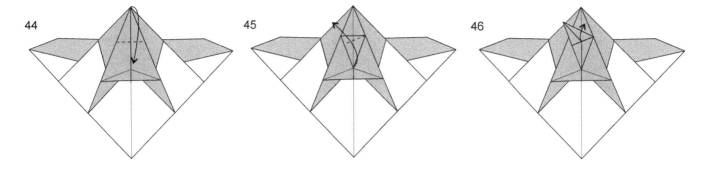

44

45

46

47

Swivel fold the flap over.

48

49

50

51

Shift the flap up.

52

Pull the trapped paper from underneath out.

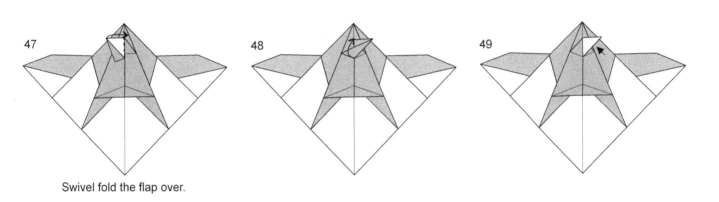

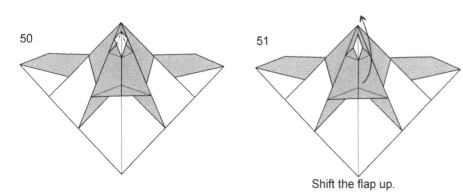

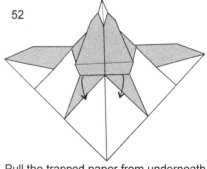

51

53

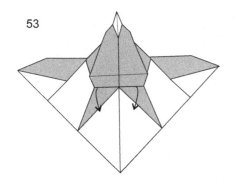

54

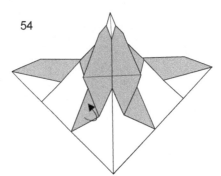

Wrap the layer from behind around.

55

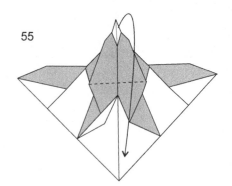

56

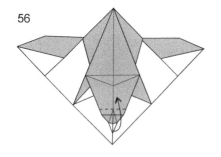

57

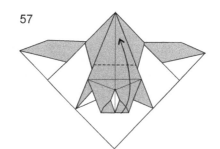

58

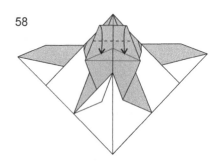

59

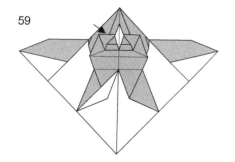

Inside reverse fold the edges in.

60

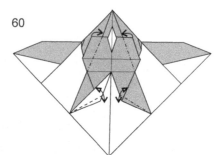

Fold the excess layers in, then fold and unfold ⅓ of the bottom edges.

61

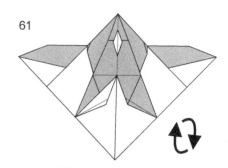

Turn the model over.

62

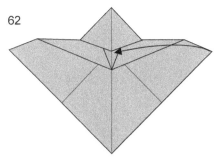

Open the side of the model.

63

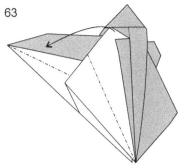

Inside reverse fold the edge in and swing the trapped paper out as shown.

64

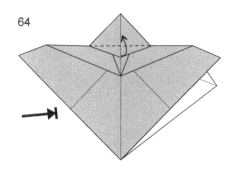

Fold the top area up, then repeat steps 59–61 to this side.

65

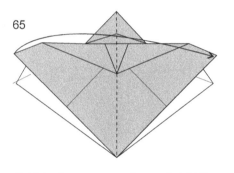

Fold the layer over and squash fold the area at the top as shown.

66

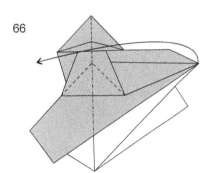

Keeping the fold you just made, return the model to step 62.

67

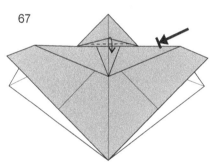

First fold the small area down, then repeat steps 62–64 to this side.

68

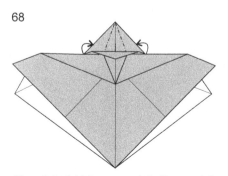

Mountain fold the areas into the model.

69

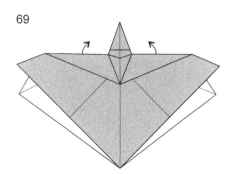

Fold the edges made in step 63 up.

70

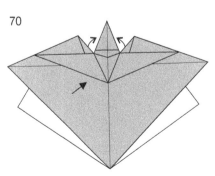

Closed sink the area, then swivel fold the inner paper up as shown.

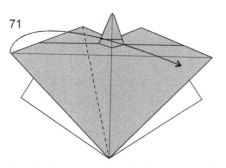

71

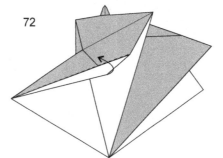

72

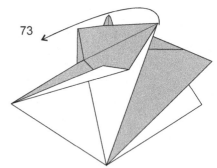

73

Fold the layer over. You will have to perform
a double swivel fold.

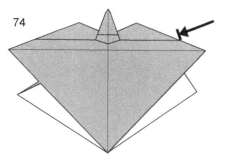

74

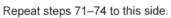

Repeat steps 71–74 to this side.

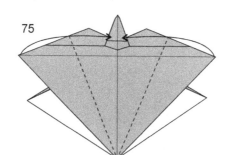

75

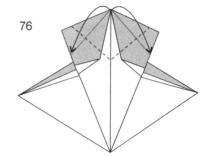

76

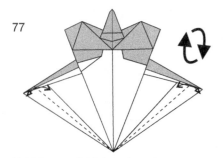

77

Fold then unfold the edges in,
then turn the model over.

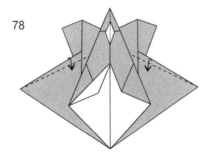

78

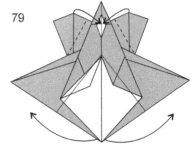

79

Fold the top edges in as shown.
Inside reverse fold the rear
flaps out.

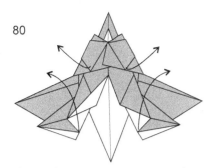

80 Swivel fold the top edges out to form the canard wings. Open out the rear flaps.

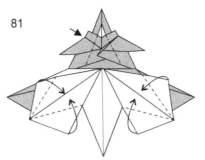

81 Mountain fold the edges under the canard wings, then swivel fold the flaps at the bottom in as shown.

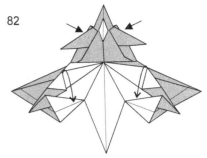

82 Place the layers into the fuselage then close the bottom flaps.

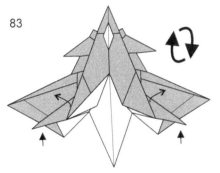

83 Slide the edges of the stabilizers out so that the edge created meets the line behind. Finally turn the model over.

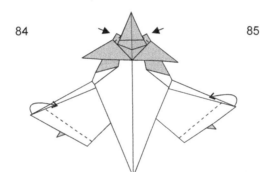

84 Swivel fold the edge in. Fold the small edges in the air intakes. Inside reverse fold the tips of the canard wings.

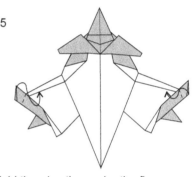

85 Fold the wing tips under the flaps as shown.

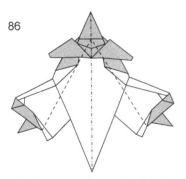

86 Jet fold the model and pull out the layer of paper under the nose.

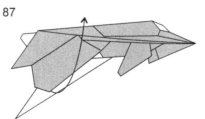

87 Fold the wings up.

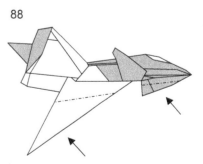

88 Inside reverse fold the flap in. Inside reverse fold the area under the nose.

89

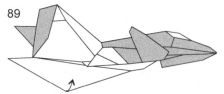

Wrap the paper around.

90

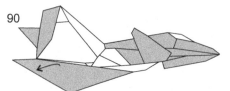

Shift the paper over.

91

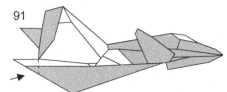

Inside reverse fold the edge in.

92

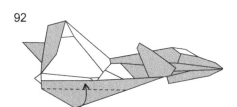

93

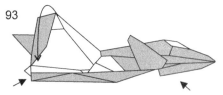

Round the afterburners, pop out the
air intakes, and fold the wings down.

94

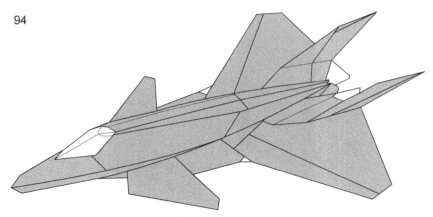

Give this plane a hard throw.

F-35 LIGHTNING

The F-35 has been developed as a multi-role fifth-generation fighter. Its roles include air superiority and ground attack. This fighter has been introduced into service recently, and has been exported to close allies of the United States. It has three versions, one for the Air Force, one for the Navy, and one for the Marines, which has short takeoff and landing abilities.

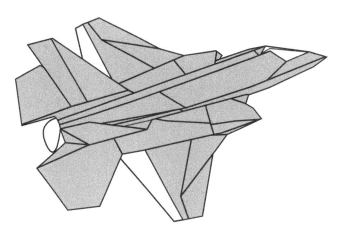

Use a 13-inch-square sheet of foil paper.

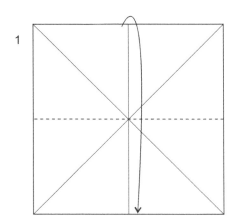

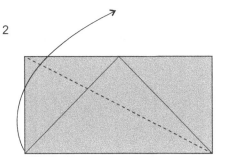

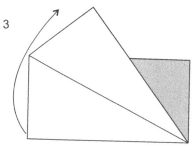

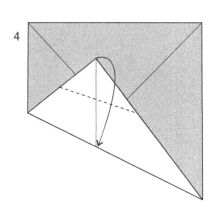

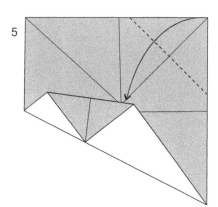

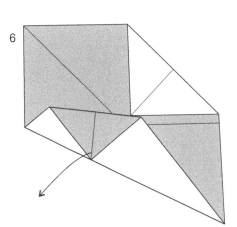

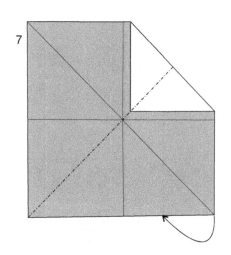

7

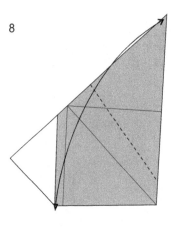

8

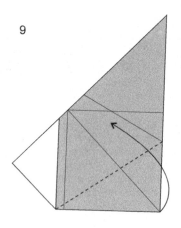

9

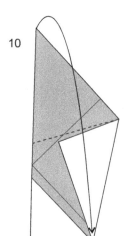

10

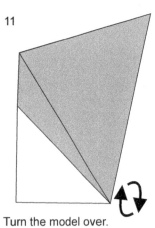

11

Turn the model over.

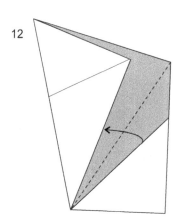

12

Fold the edge over to the line shown.

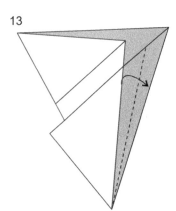

13

Fold the edge over to the line shown.

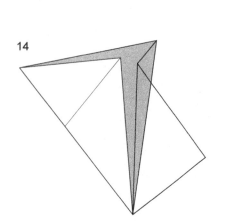

14

Return the paper to step 10.

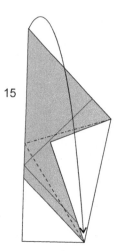

15

Open the paper along the creases shown.

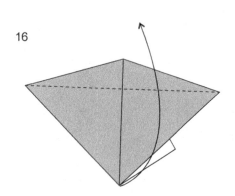

16

58

17

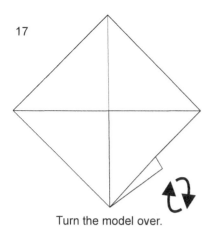

Turn the model over.

18

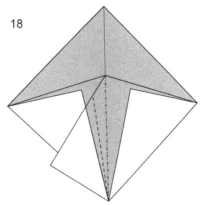

Inside reverse fold the edge along the creases shown.

19

Turn the model over.

20

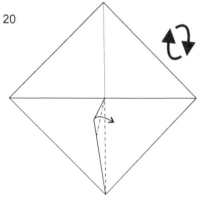

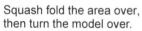

Squash fold the area over, then turn the model over.

21

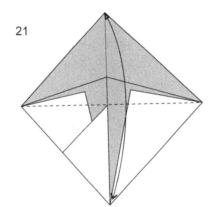

Fold then unfold the flap.

22

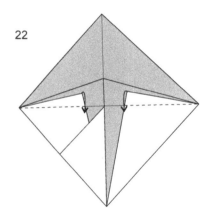

23

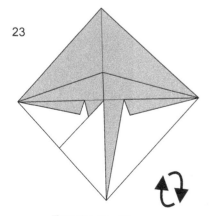

Turn the model over.

24

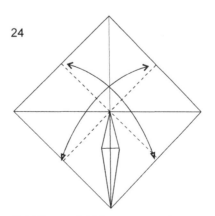

Fold then unfold the creases shown.

25

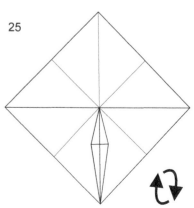

Turn the model over.

59

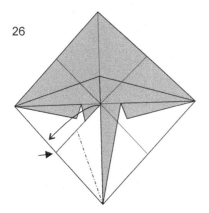

26

Inside reverse fold the edge and swing the layer of trapped paper out.

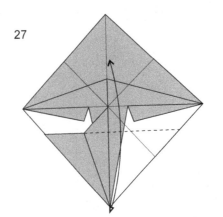

27

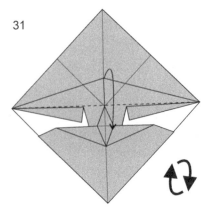

28

Fold the area on the small triangle out, then swing the layers up as shown in step 29.

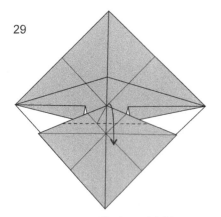

29

Perform a modified petal fold.

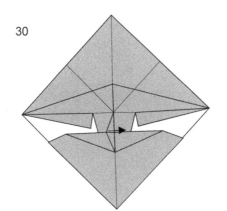

30

Pull the trapped paper out.

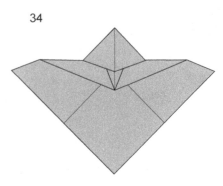

31

Fold the flap down, then turn the model over.

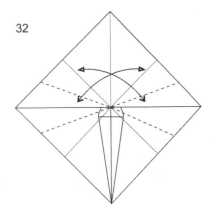

32

Fold then unfold the creases shown.

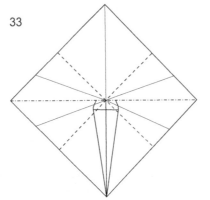

33

Form a preliminary fold.

34

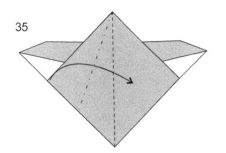

35

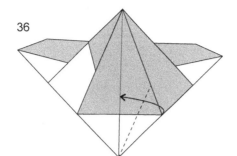

36

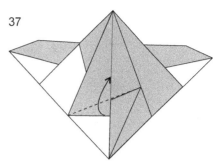

37

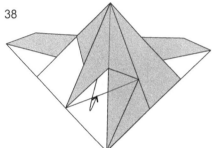

38

Fold the edge underneath.

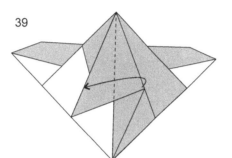

39

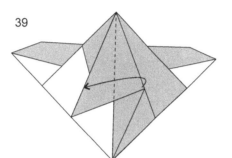

40

Fold the flap up and swivel the edge over.

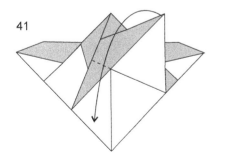

41

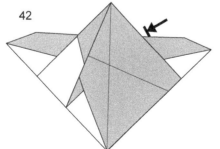

42

Repeat steps 35–42 to this side.

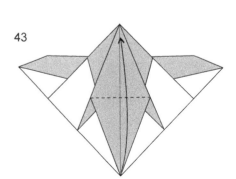

43

44

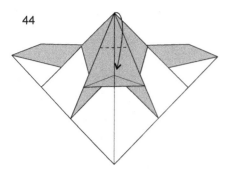

45

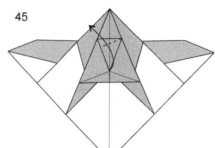

46

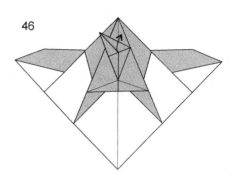

47

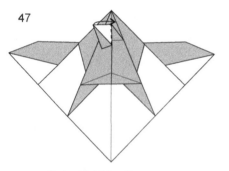

Swivel fold the flap over.

48

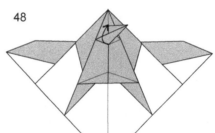

49

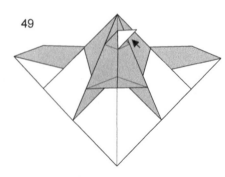

50

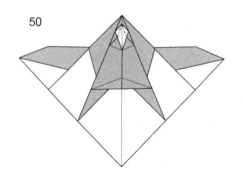

51

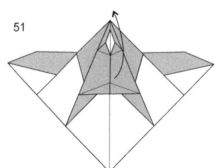

Shift the flap up.

52

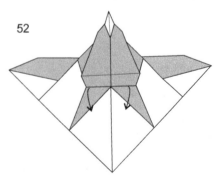

Pull the trapped paper from underneath out.

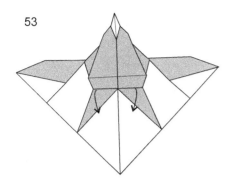

53

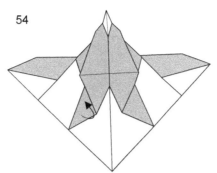

54

Wrap the layer from behind around.

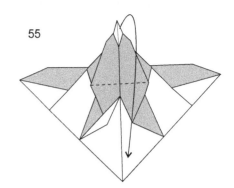

55

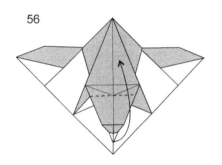

56

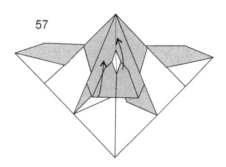

57

Slide the area up as shown until the
edges line up as shown in step 58.

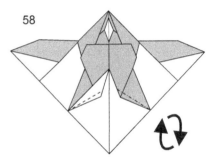

58

Fold then unfold the edges as shown,
then turn the model over.

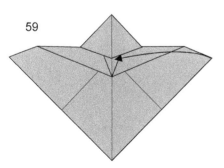

59

Open the side of the model.

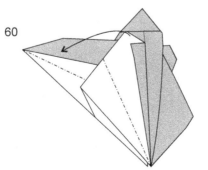

60

Inside reverse fold the edge in and
swing the trapped paper out as shown.

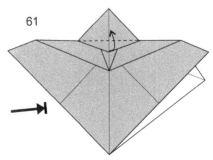

61

Fold the top area up then
repeat steps 59–61 to this side.

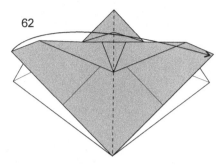

62

Fold the layer over and squash fold the area at the top as shown.

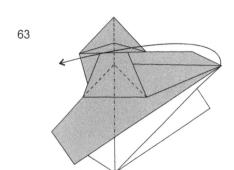

63

Keeping the fold you just made return the model to step 62.

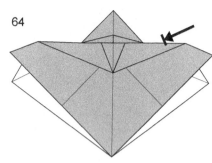

64

Repeat steps 62–64 to this side.

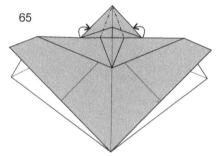

65

Inside reverse fold the edges in.

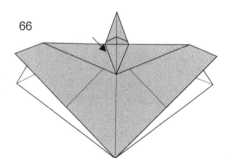

66

Open sink this area.

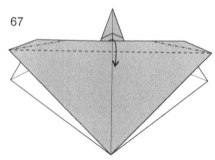

67

Fold the edges down and squash fold the corners.

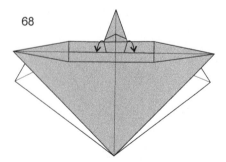

68

Fold the small inner corners down as shown.

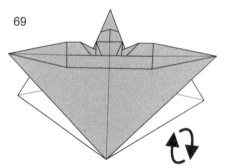

69

Turn the model over.

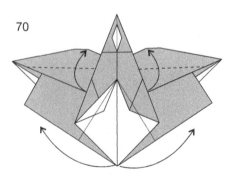

70

Fold the flaps out from the center point and perpendicular to the bottom edge. Then fold the edges up to the corners as shown.

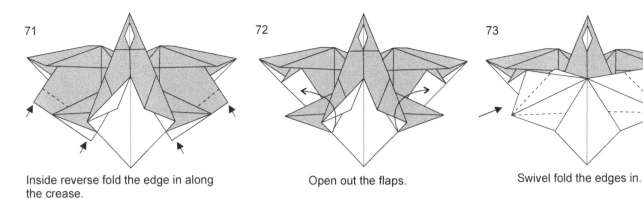

71 Inside reverse fold the edge in along the crease.

72 Open out the flaps.

73 Swivel fold the edges in.

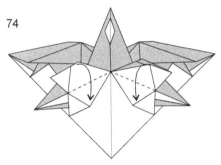
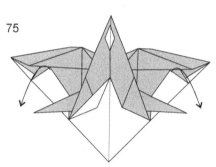
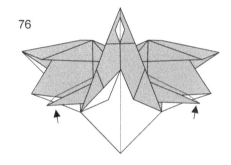

74 Close the flaps.

75 Swivel the edges out as far as they will go.

76 Slide the top layers up to the intersections shown.

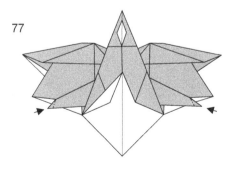
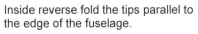
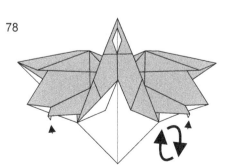
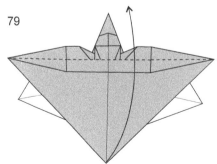

77 Inside reverse fold the tips parallel to the edge of the fuselage.

78 Fold the tips in, then turn the model over.

79

80

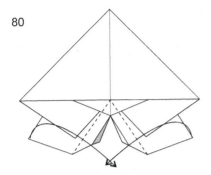

Inside reverse fold the flaps down as far as they can go.

81

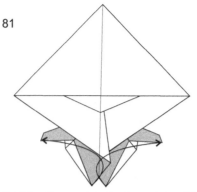

Fold the flaps out to the far points of the stabilizers.

82

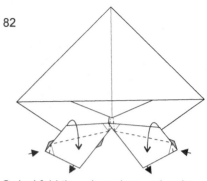

Swivel fold the edges down using the creases shown as a guide, fold the small tips in, and pull the trapped paper from behind out as shown.

83

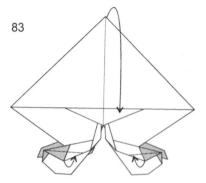

Fold the edges in, then fold the large flap down.

84

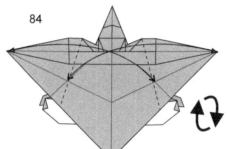

Fold then unfold the wings to the intersections shown, then turn the model over.

85

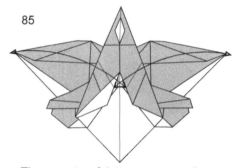

There are two faint creases, use the intersection shown to fold and unfold the wingtips.

86

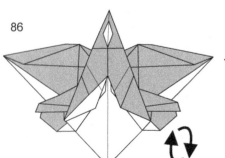

Turn the model over.

87

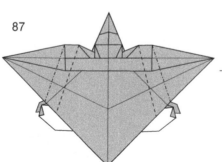

Pleat the wings in using the creases you just made.

88

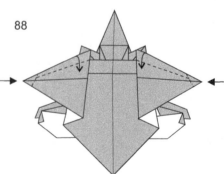

Using the creases inside reverse fold the tips in, then swivel fold the edges down.

89

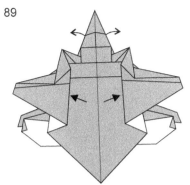

Closed sink the edges behind the layers beneath it. Bring the edges you inside reverse folded from earlier out.

90

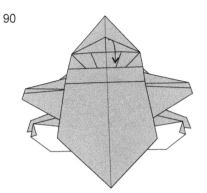

Fold this layer back down.

91

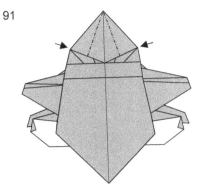

Inside reverse fold the edges back.

92

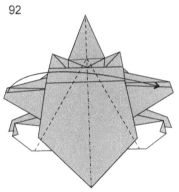

Jet fold the model as shown.

93

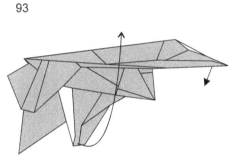

Fold the wings up and fold the excess paper under the nose out.

94

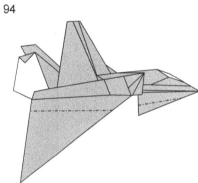

First lock the model together by placing the flap inside the pocket made earlier and folding them over into thirds, inside reverse fold the tail up and thin the nose out.

95

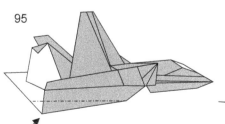

Fold the edges in as shown.

96

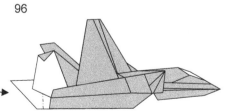

Inside reverse fold the edge in.

97

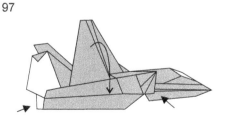

Round the afterburner, position the wings, and shape the air intakes.

67

98

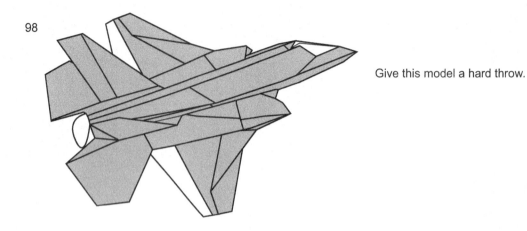

Give this model a hard throw.

SUKHOI SU-57

The SU-57 started development in 2002 as a joint project with India and Russia. India later backed out of the program. It is the first Russian stealth fighter to be produced, and it was designed to be an air superiority fighter. It has seen service in Syria.

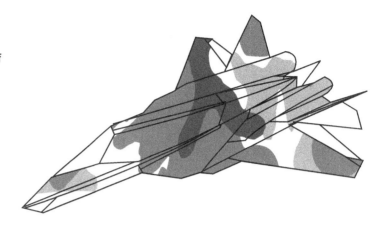

Use a 13-inch-square sheet of foil paper.

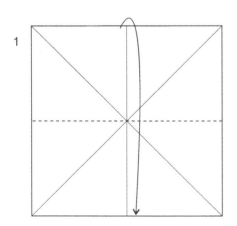

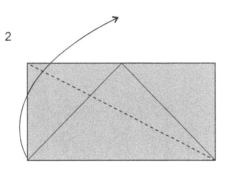

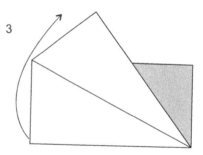

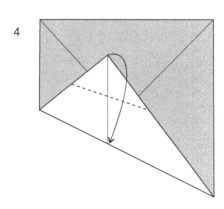

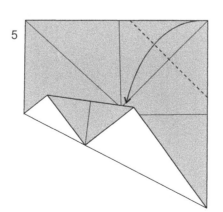

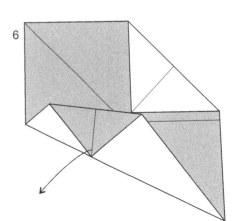

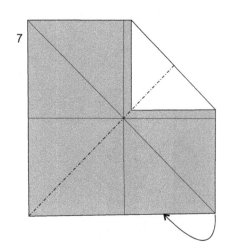

7

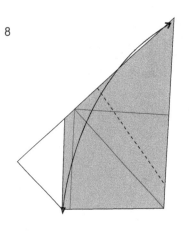

8

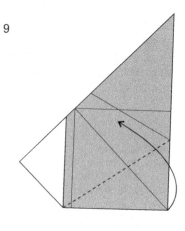

9

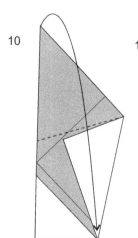

10

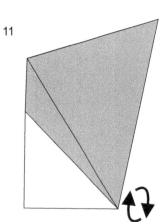

11

Turn the model over.

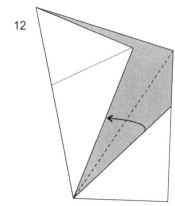

12

Fold the edge over to the line shown.

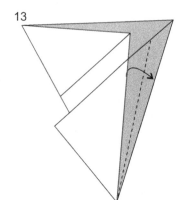

13

Fold the edge over to the line shown.

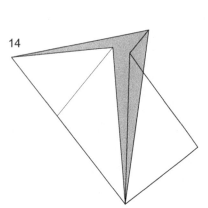

14

Return the paper to step 10.

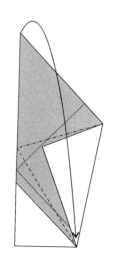

15

Open the paper along the creases shown.

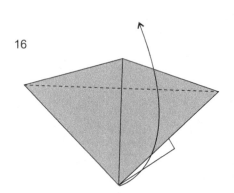

16

17

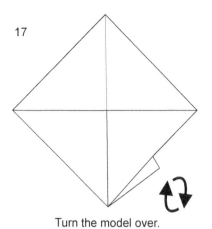

Turn the model over.

18

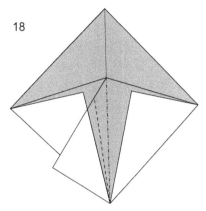

Inside reverse fold the edge along the creases shown.

19

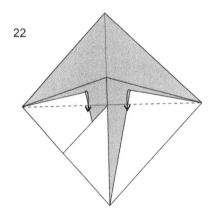

Turn the model over.

20

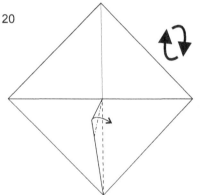

Squash fold the area over, then turn the model over.

21

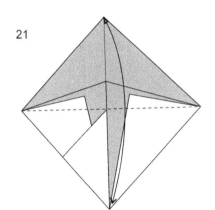

Fold then unfold the flap.

22

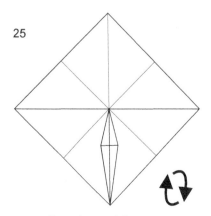

23

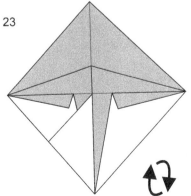

Turn the model over.

24

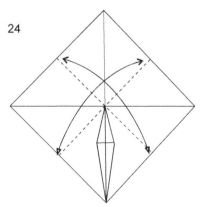

Fold then unfold the creases shown.

25

Turn the model over.

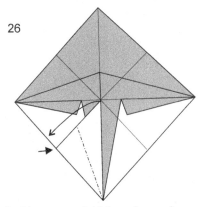

26

Inside reverse fold the edge and swing the layer of trapped paper out.

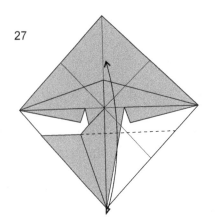

27

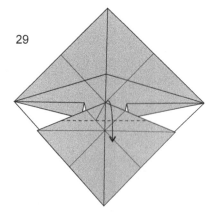

28

Fold the area on the small triangle out then swing the layers up as shown in step 29.

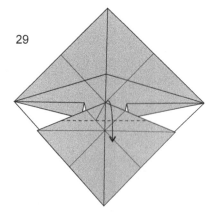

29

Perform a modified petal fold.

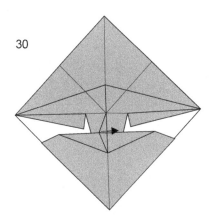

30

Pull the trapped paper out.

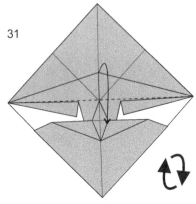

31

Fold the flap down then turn the model over.

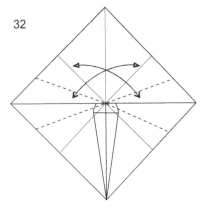

32

Fold then unfold the creases shown.

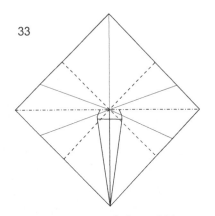

33

Form a preliminary fold.

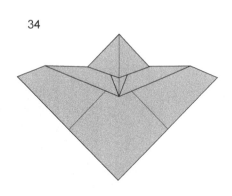

34

35

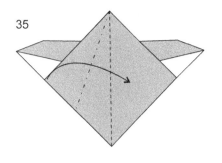

36

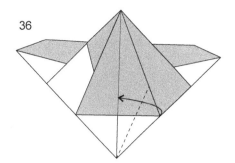

37

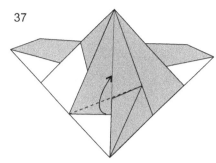

38

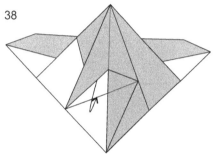

Fold the edge underneath.

39

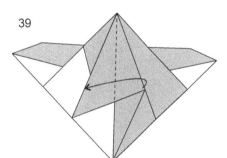

40

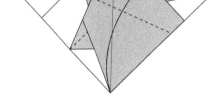

Fold the flap up and swivel the edge over.

41

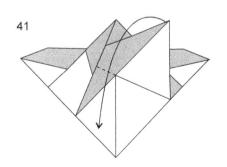

42

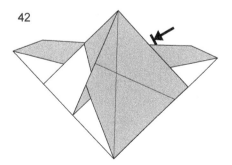

Repeat steps 35–42 to this side.

43

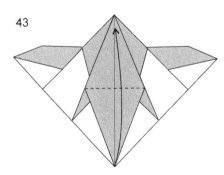

73

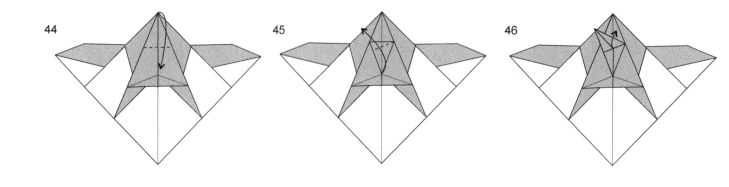

47   48   49

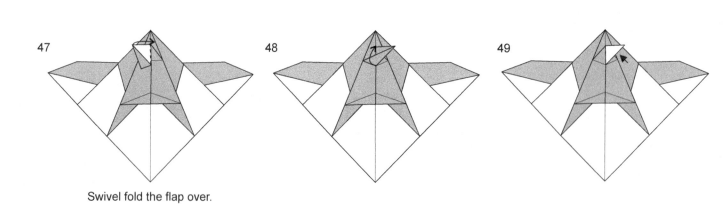

Swivel fold the flap over.

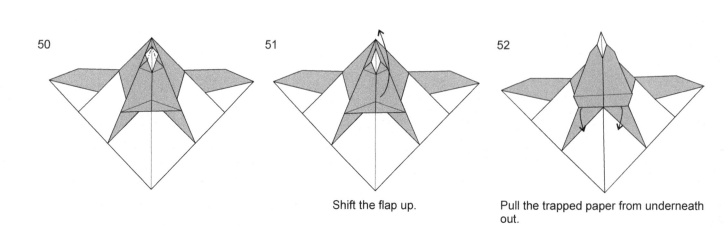

Shift the flap up.

Pull the trapped paper from underneath out.

53

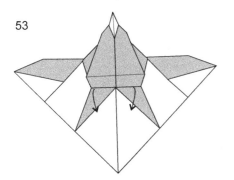

54

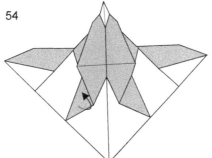

Wrap the layer from behind around.

55

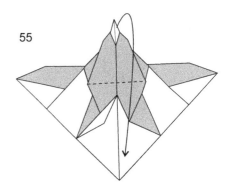

56

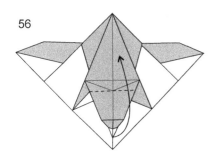

57

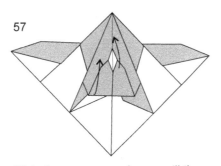

Slide the area up as shown until the
edges line up as shown in step 58.

58

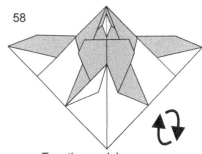

Turn the model over.

59

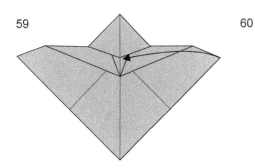

Open the side of the model.

60

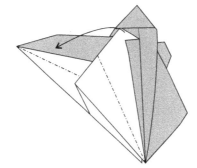

Inside reverse fold the edge in and
swing the trapped paper out as shown.

61

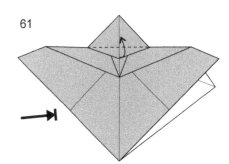

Fold the top area up then
repeat steps 59–61 to this side.

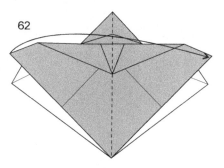

62

Fold the layer over and squash fold the area at the top as shown.

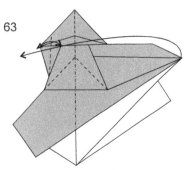

63

First fold and unfold the small side in. Keeping the fold you just made, return the model to step 62.

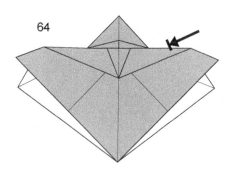

64

Repeat steps 62–64 to this side.

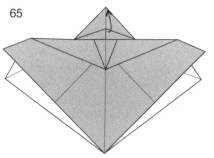

65

Pull the edge up and perform a modified petal fold.

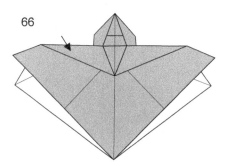

66

Closed sink the large triangular area in.

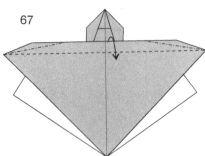

67

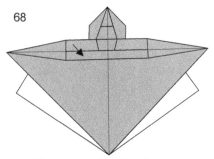

68

Closed sink the edge in.

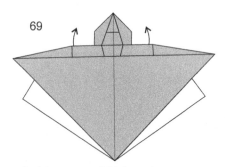

69

Inside reverse fold the edges made in step 63 up.

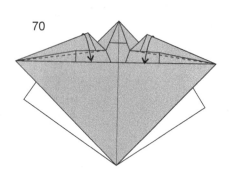

70

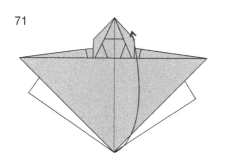

71

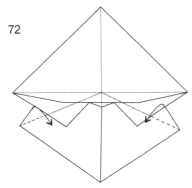

72

Slide the paper down as shown.

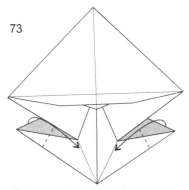

73

Fold the edges in on the
lines shown.

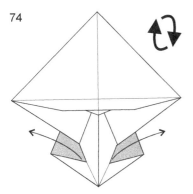

74

Fold the flaps out, then turn
the model over.

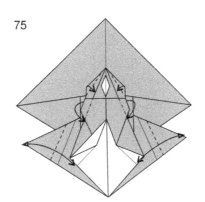

75

Fold the small edges of the
triangular area in. Fold the
sides of the excess paper in.
Fold then unfold the flaps.

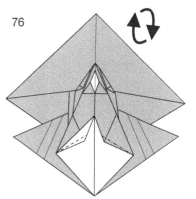

76

Fold then unfold the edges
of the area shown in thirds.
This will become the
locking mechanism. Turn
the model over.

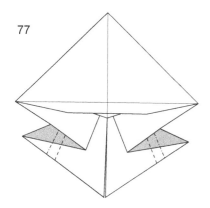

77

Inside reverse fold the flaps
along the creases.

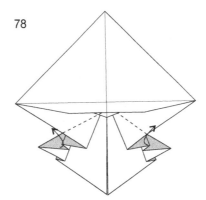

78

Fold the top layers up.

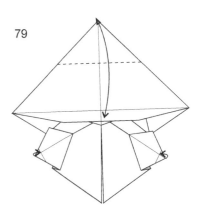

79

Fold the small tips in to the
intersections shown. Fold
then unfold the flap as shown.

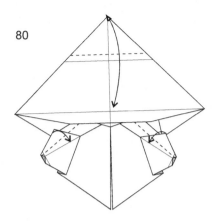

80

Fold then unfold the flap as shown. Fold the edges of the flaps in as shown.

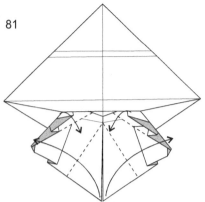

81

Fold the top of the flaps down the fold the bottom flaps over perpendicular.

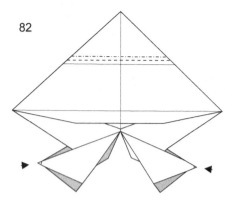

82

Pleat the top flap using the creases. Inside reverse fold the small tips on the rear flaps in.

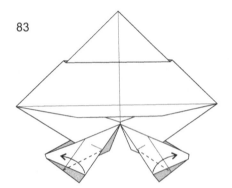

83

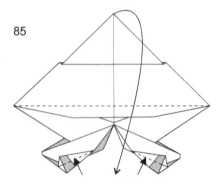

84

Fold the edges over using the inner edges and the edges behind.

85

Move the paper under the layer behind it, then fold the top flap down.

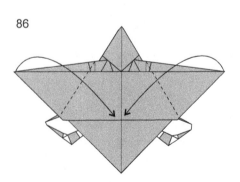

86

Using the small line on the top edge and the leading edge of the tailfin, fold the flaps in.

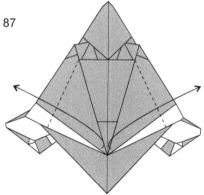

87

Fold the wings out starting from the intersection shown, then fold the bottom edge perpendicular to the edge.

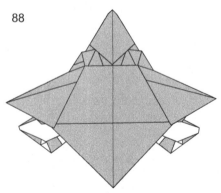

88

Inside reverse fold the wings using the creases you just made.

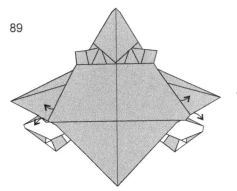

89

Pull the excess paper down and out to enlarge the wings.

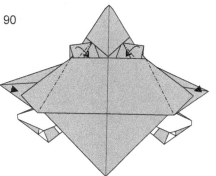

90

Swivel fold the excess layers at the top in, then push the excess layers on the wings in.

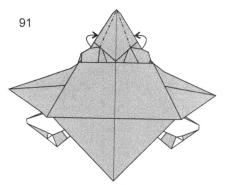

91

Mountain fold the edges into the fuselage, then turn the model over.

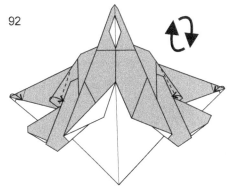

92

Inside reverse fold the wingtips in, then fold the small excess paper on the wings in, then turn the model over.

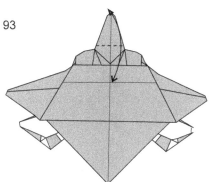

93

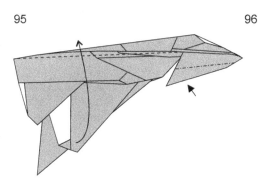

94

Perform a jet fold but fold the excess layer under the nose out as shown in step 95.

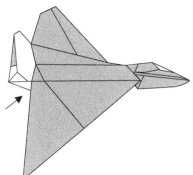

95

Inside reverse fold the flap underneath the nose in and fold the wings up.

96

Insert the one flap into the other then roll them over using the creases made previously. This locks the model together.

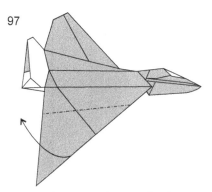

97

Inside reverse fold the flap in.

98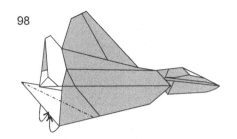

99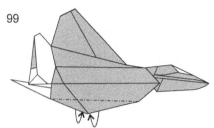

100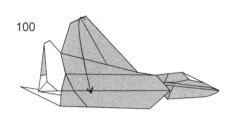

101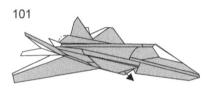

Round the afterburners and shape
the air intakes.

102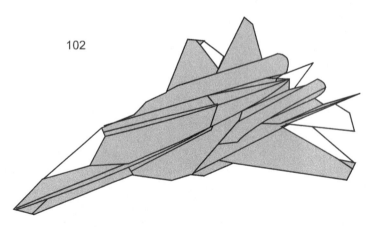

To fly this aircraft, grab the keel and give it a firm throw.
Once properly balanced, it can fly up to 115 feet.